ARMADA
THE TERRIFYING QUEST

ARKSEARCH

THE TERRIFYING QUEST

ALLEN ROBERTS

MONARCH
Crowborough

First published 1994

British Library Cataloguing in Publication Data
A catalogue record for this book is available from the British Library

ISBN: 1 85424 273 3

Designed and produced in England for
MONARCH PUBLICATIONS
The Broadway, Crowborough, East Sussex TN6 1HQ by
Nuprint Ltd, Station Road, Harpenden, Herts AL5 4SE.

CONTENTS

The term *Arksearch* used as the title of this book has no connection with any organisation of the same or similar name.

FOREWORD

I wish to thank the many people who helped not only to make this book possible but also to ensure my survival and the opportunity to write it.

- The numerous researchers who since 1948 have made their findings available—in particular Ron Wyatt, without whose freely-shared information and encouragement I would never have been privileged even to be involved in the project that took me to Turkey. I have come to value Ron's and his wife Mary Nell's wonderful friendship and their outstanding insights into things archaeological.

- My four fellow hostages for their friendship and support. Being at gunpoint for three weeks gives one a splendid opportunity to find out who one's real friends are. My thanks to Ron, Richard, Marvin and the coercively co-opted fifth member of our team, Gary.

- Those who represent the government of Turkey; those at the Turkish Embassies in both Canberra and London and also at the Consulate in Sydney. Without their active support, our applications to investigate the site and to discuss plans to develop it with the appropriate Turkish Ministries would never have occurred. The advice and help given by these officials have also made an invaluable contribution to this book.

- On behalf of the five of us who were kidnapped, heartfelt thanks to the Government of Turkey and in particular to the large number of soldiers who made such massive, costly and dangerous efforts to ensure that we survived the experiences I have recounted.

- The Australian Ambassador to Turkey, Mr Don Witherford and his Consul, Mr Allen Williams, whom he released to liaise with the Turkish authorities when we were missing and even to assist in their search for us.

- Tony Collins and his wife Jane at Monarch for their encouragement to me to press on towards the publication of this book, and especially their patience and forbearance throughout the time I was writing it.

- Arthur and Vivienne Roderick for their hospitality during the several months when I was writing it, and to Steven Cowley for assisting with the typing of the manuscript.

- Historian and scientist friends who took time to review my manuscript and made many valuable suggestions.

- While I acknowledge the help and encouragement of so many in the writing of this book, the responsibility for what is contained in it belongs to me and not to any other individual or organisation.

- And I wish to thank my wife Margaret who throughout the time I was missing continued with great courage, along with the rest of my family and friends, to pray for our safety and release.

When that release came, I was reported in the press as saying 'Thank God I'm free!' I still do, and have written this book that God might be honoured and if he allows it, might enable me yet to have some small part in answering the question 'If this is not Noah's Ark, what is it?'

Allen Roberts
January 1994

CHAPTER

1

Kidnapped!

Men shouted. Women screamed.

The noise jogged me out of my cat-nap on the rear seat of our minibus.

'What on earth is going on?' I asked myself. 'And why have we stopped on this lonely road?'

I sat up and looked around. It was too dark to see anything outside—except a tourist bus in the blaze of our headlights, with my travelling companions silhouetted against it.

The shouting and the noise of many voices grew louder.

In spite of the darkness outside, one thing was certain. This was not just another of those routine police checks we'd all become used to on the country roads of Eastern Turkey.

The possibility that this might have been a traffic accident never even crossed my mind. There was something about the shouting of those rough male voices that was disturbingly different. It was distinctly menacing; calculated to engender fear and panic.

Suddenly, a man I couldn't see began to yell at us through our front window. The phrase sounded like Kurdish. It was repeated several times with increasing volume and insistence.

Ron Wyatt, our 228 lb archaeologist, imperturbable as usual, simply drawled in his deep Southern accent, 'I think they want us to get out with our hands up.'

The side door of our minibus rolled open with a hollow rumble and clunk.

Each of us groped his way towards the opening. As we stepped down on to the roadside with our hands above our heads, another vehicle pulled up behind our minibus. Its headlights bathed everything in light. In one moment all our queries were answered.

Ron Wyatt
at gunpoint

We were being held at gunpoint by a band of guerrillas— almost certainly Kurdish.

They seemed to be everywhere; maybe a dozen or so of them, all garbed in 'guerilla-come-dressed-as-you-shabbily-please' costumes and all armed to the teeth with powerful automatic weapons. Their guns included such a wide range of makes and models that I was sure they must have been stolen—perhaps even plundered from soldiers they'd killed.

I could still hear the distraught voices of women and children; their crying and pleading seemed to come from the tourist bus at the head of the road-block.

The man who had his gun trained on us was young; twenty at the most, I reckoned. In appearance he was typically Kurdish. His features were coarse but strong and manly. Like all his comrades he was bare-headed. His hair was short, thick and jet-black like his moustache. His chin sported the dark stubble of a two-week growth. Like most Kurds, he was of medium height, very fit and rangy. (There seem to be fewer overweight male Kurds than overweight male Westerners.)

He wore a grubby old khaki jacket that hung open at the front. His loose-fitting grey trousers were gathered at the waist and ankles, baggy at the knees. Around his waist was a wide brass-buckled military belt. Attached to it, I could see a number of black leather magazine pouches and hand-grenades. Strung from his left shoulder to his right hip was a bandolier that contained fifty or sixty bronze-coloured rounds of .308 calibre ammunition.

Young and scruffy as he appeared, one got the impression that he was both expert and practised in this guerrilla business.

The sub-machine-gun that hung so easily from the strap over his right shoulder had a kind of 'lived-with' look to it. He used it to wave the four of us along, with our guide and driver, towards the rear bumper of our minibus. As he did so, I noticed that his gun did not have a wooden butt. Instead it had something similar in shape but made of steel—a kind of hollow frame.

I was born and raised in kangaroo country, the outback of Western New South Wales, and had never been convinced that these mere steel outlines could belong to real guns. But suddenly he pointed the thing directly at me, and my focus of attention was immediately transferred to that little hole at the business end of the barrel. I was instantly convinced that this was indeed a real gun.

Strange how rapidly one can change one's opinion about some things.

In the next few moments Ron, Marvin, Richard and myself found ourselves surrounded by several of our captors.

They began to interrogate us in Kurdish. This wasn't much use, since none of us could understand or speak the language. It soon became clear however that they were very keen to know from which country we'd come and what we were doing in Turkey.

Ron, Richard and Marvin somehow managed to convey the information that they'd come to do archaeological work. I heard them mention in this regard Nuh'un Gemisi, the reason for our archaeological trip to Turkey. When they identified themselves as Americans, I sensed a reaction that was not exactly friendly. In the comments which followed, the name 'George Bush' was mentioned, and the tone became distinctly hostile.

On previous visits to Eastern Turkey I had detected a certain amount of anti-American feeling. However, I had assumed that America's role against Saddam Hussein in the Gulf War and its aftermath might have changed all that. I had also assumed that for the same reason Australians like me might be seen as friends; people to be helped rather than hindered or harmed. So when they turned their attention to me, I tried to explain, in the best Turkish I could muster, my country of origin and my reason for being in Turkey.

'*Benim* Allen Roberts . . . Doctor . . . *archaeologie—ben Avustralya.*'

The man who seemed to be in charge responded immediately—but not in the way I had hoped. His eyes blazed with anger. Then, with his fist clenched and thumb extended towards himself, he jabbed his breast shouting, '*Kurdi! Kurdi!*'

What had I said that had so offended him?

I stood there, not knowing what to say or do. He spat out the words again: '*Kurdi! Kurdi!*'

Then it suddenly dawned on me. In speaking Turkish, I had inadvertently made a serious (and dangerous) political *faux pas*. As recently as two years ago there had been a Turkish law forbidding Kurds to speak their native tongue. Although this legislation had been recently repealed, Kurdish feelings on the issue still ran high and were now, it appeared, expressing themselves in a sort of retaliation. It went something like this: if a Turkish regime can pass a law to ban Kurdish, then a Kurdish regime—under local guerrilla law—can ban Turkish. I had been told, in no uncertain manner, that the only acceptable communication medium between us was to be Kurdish.

This was one of those rare situations in which one can truly say, 'I was left speechless.'

At this point, Richard Rives, our huge boyish-faced travel director from North Carolina, tried to help. His six-foot-four bulk towering over everyone, he laid his hand on my shoulder. Then, in a voice that had the twangy, nasal musicality of a Jew's harp (and with about as little jaw movement as it takes to play one) he said,

'Dr Roberts is a professor—he's a *professor*!'

For some reason, this seemed to please them and they repeated

Richard Rivers

the word 'professor' as though they were delighted to have captured one.

To my relief, our guide and long-time friend Dilaver suddenly appeared and began to engage the guerrillas in conversation.

'At last', I thought, 'someone will be able to explain to them who we really are and that we are not here to do anyone any harm.'

The conversation between Dilaver and the guerrillas continued at a volume which, in most Western countries, would signify a heated argument. In Eastern Turkey, however, ordinary conversations are often carried on at extraordinary volume levels—on the basis, presumably, that if something is worth saying, it's worth saying loud.

Dilaver turned to us and, using the phrase much employed by those in Turkey who have limited English, said,

'No problem! No problem!'

He was obviously trying to reassure us. His words suggested that we'd soon all be back in our minibus and on our way. However, there was something in the pitch of his voice that suggested otherwise.

Suddenly, without notice, the guerrillas began to herd us back towards the front of the road-block. Still under guard and with our hands above our heads, Marvin Wilson and I were made to stand in front of our minibus. (Marvin, a man in his early fifties, bright-eyed, dark-complexioned and athletic in his white leather jogging shoes, was a leading business consultant from Texas.)

Marvin Wilson

We were suddenly joined by Dilaver. Like everybody else, he was still under guard. Any talking between us was risky. Nonetheless, he ran the risk.

'Dr Roberts,' he said, in his husky Kurdish voice, 'these men—terrorist—PKK!' He pronounced the initials in the Kurdish manner: 'Pay Kar Kar.'

'OK,' I responded, quickly nodding my head to show I understood.

Once more Dilaver sought to reassure us—'No problem. No problem!'—and once more I was not reassured. Within seconds, and without warning, Dilaver was led away by his guard towards the other end of our minibus.

'Where are they taking him?' I wondered. 'And where are Ron and Richard—and our driver?'

I was beginning to be concerned for them—as no doubt they were for us. My concern was increased by Dilaver's information that these guerrillas were members of the PKK—in English, People's Workers' Party—which was a Kurdish Marxist movement banned by the Turkish government as a terrorist organisation.

I could still hear a good deal of shouting from behind our bus. It was not possible to see what was going on, for it had now grown very dark.

The mountain air was becoming quite chilly. I had seriously injured my left ankle several years ago in an accident; as a result the circulation in that leg had been impaired. The drop in temperature was causing my toes to go numb, so to get my circulation going, I began to move my feet up and down. Fine dust from the road smouldered upwards through the shafts of light thrown by the headlights of our bus.

As I stared into the night I began to turn things over in my mind.

'So they're PKK,' I mused.

I was not really surprised. I knew that the PKK had been active in this province, particularly around the town of Bingol which was to have been our first stop on this investigative field trip.

We were aware that encounters with the PKK usually occurred at night. With that in mind we had planned to complete this first leg of our journey during daylight hours. However, due to a number of unexpected delays, here we were, in the very region where guerrilla activity was common, just after sunset.

'Well,' I thought, 'that's all water under the bridge now. No point in mulling over the unchangeable past. The important question now is, "What are we going to do, here in the present?" '

Unfortunately there didn't seem to be much mileage in that question either. A quick glance at our guard's Russian Kalashnikov with its curved magazine clip convinced me that none of the standard adventure-film solutions would be appropriate right now. Making a break for it into the mountains, driving our minibus around or through the road block, overpowering the guards—somehow none of these heroic strategies recommended themselves.

Clearly we had no control over the present situation. The PKK had taken the initiative away from us. As far as our future went, they seemed to have that pretty well under control too. It really depended on what they planned to do with us.

'What are their plans for this operation?' I asked myself.

I knew that over recent years, the PKK had become a formidable military strike-force in Eastern Turkey. Most of their operations had been carefully organised and skilfully executed. As a result of their hit-and-run attacks, thousands of lives had been lost within a period of only a few years. Political commentators had expressed the fear that these conflicts might escalate into a bloody civil war throughout Turkey.

Yet I didn't think that this particular operation had been designed to lead to a shoot-out with Turkish government forces, the military or *gendarma*. Even so it had the potential to become one; all it would take would be for an army truck or police car to come around that bend and the shooting would start.

'No,' I reasoned, 'this little sortie has been planned for some other purpose.

'Perhaps,' I conjectured, 'it's some sort of armed hold-up to steal money or goods which could be used to buy arms.'

However I doubted that this was the case either. None of us had been searched, no luggage had been ransacked, no wallets had been taken—either from us or from anyone else, as far as I knew.

'This is not a highway robbery job,' I concluded.

Without warning another thought came into my mind—dark, clammy, uninvited.

'Could this whole thing be a reprisal exercise?' Before I could control it, my mind took the thought and ran with it.

'Maybe their purpose is to exact the death penalty for real or imagined grievances against the Kurdish people.'

Firing squads carrying out such aims were not infrequent in various parts of the world, including the Middle East. Furthermore, all the necessary conditions for such a capital-punishment exercise seemed to have been met.

First, the place was ideal: a fairly well-travelled country road with a choice of vehicles to intercept—plenty of potential victims too, and a bus-load of witnesses to tell the world that these death-dealing terrorists meant business.

Secondly, the wild mountainous terrain surrounding the spot would also be ideal for such a grisly scenario—plenty of places to hide in beforehand and withdraw to afterwards. Also this narrow road that wound through the pass would be easy to block off. One vehicle parked across it would do the job. I could see that they'd actually done this, by using what looked like a white Renault 16 sedan.

Thirdly, they'd captured four people from the Western world, possibly more. To execute some of them would be an ideal move if they wanted to work off a grudge against President George Bush or Prime Minister Bob Hawke for their pro-Turkish alliances. Perhaps Marvin and I, in being made to stand apart from the others, had already been singled out to represent our countries in this macabre manner.

As these thoughts began to surface, I realised that to allow my imagination to develop them further would be foolish and dangerous. Looking for evidence to back up possible bad scenarios is the first step to losing control. So when we were joined by a middle-aged Turkish gentleman with his fingers laced together on the top of his balding head, I stifled the thought that maybe he was going to be shot with us as a collaborator.

The din of voices at the rear of our minibus suddenly increased. I fancied I could hear Ron's voice in the hubbub.

Our guards beckoned to us, so Marvin and I moved towards them where they stood on the edge of the roadway.

'This could be it,' I thought.

I looked down into the dry gully that ran alongside the road. As I did so, the execution scenario began to take visual form on the silent screen of my mind. There in the space of a few seconds, I saw Ron, Richard, Marvin and myself being goaded by the guns of a hastily-formed firing squad down into that dry gully. I saw our awkward arms, jerkily trying to maintain our balance as we slid and stumbled down over the loose stones and dirt. No sound-track; no dramatic volley of shots; no more moving images. Just our silent bodies in that gully.

This was not the first time I had faced death. In the Middle East, such lethal situations can and do suddenly arise, without warning.

What does one do in a situation like this?

One does what many—if not most—people do in such a situation; one prays.

I had barely begun, when I was grabbed and hustled with Marvin to the rear of our minibus yet again. To my relief, I saw Ron and Richard standing there. They appeared to be unharmed but were being yelled at by the man in charge; a clean-shaven young man in his late twenties. A torrent of Kurdish words poured from his mouth, as he repeatedly jabbed his gun towards the rear door of our minibus. Ron opened it, revealing several items of our luggage stacked behind the back seat.

After more shouting and gun-waving at our luggage and at us, we realised that we were being ordered to open our cases. This very vocal young man seemed interested in one particular case;

an aluminium one that belonged to Ron. When Ron indicated that he had no key on him with which to open it, the gun-prodding and yelling became almost frenzied. I wondered for a moment whether his anger was real or simulated. If real, then the man was positively dangerous; and very possibly capable of uncontrolled violence. If it was simulated then it was simply part of the guerrilla's psychological stock-in-trade; terror tactics to intimidate us. In any case the gun he brandished so threateningly made the whole question purely academic.

As we stood there waiting for their next move, one of the men handed Ron an old pair of navy-blue trousers. He put them on over the ones he was wearing. Then they handed him an old khaki army jacket. As he slipped it on, he looked towards us, and in his deep resonant voice said,

'Looks like they plan to take me with them.'

Another guerrilla turned up with more trousers and jackets draped over his arm. He checked them for size and then started to hand them out to the rest of us. They gave me a well-worn khaki jacket that stank of stale Turkish cigarette smoke.

It seemed pretty clear that Ron was not the only one they planned to take with them.

We were all to be taken hostage. The exact purpose was not yet clear. What was clear, however, was that they didn't want us to freeze in these mountains. I viewed this as one positive aspect of an otherwise grim situation.

'The handing out of these clothes,' I thought 'would seem to indicate that we are of more use to them alive than dead.'

The execution scenario was dissolving and being replaced by the hostage one.

We all had our jackets on now, but I was still waiting for the quartermaster to issue me with my trousers. I thought I qualified for a pair, since I was wearing only thin cotton overalls which my friends called my 'boiler suit'. They were a sort of lightweight track suit; ideal on an archaeological site during Turkey's hot summer days, but quite unsuitable for the cold nights of these mountains.

One of our guards checked the thickness of my boiler-suit material for warmth. He then bent down and pulled up my left trouser leg, no doubt to ascertain the suitability of my footwear for trekking over this rugged mountain terrain.

His inspection revealed my tall saddle boots. I'd bought them from a chain-store in Nashville, Tennessee, just prior to coming to Turkey. I was quite proud of them, since they cost me only $9.00. I didn't particularly like the colour, a light tan, nor was I impressed by the fancy embroidery which so many Americans seem to go for. But I bought them on the basis that at $4.50 per boot I simply couldn't go wrong. The guard allowed the leg of my trousers to drop down again, then walked away. I assumed that like me, he thought that with those boots on, I'd be well shod.

We were both soon to be proved very wrong.

As for my extra pair of trousers, nobody offered me any. I would just have to make do, it seemed, with my boiler suit with its one thin layer of cotton.

Within a few minutes, the group began to move out. Marvin and I were taken along the edge of the road and made to stand there. Among the shouting out of final orders, I heard Dilaver's voice. No doubt he was still pleading on our behalf. He called out in a valiant attempt to reassure us that things would be all right, but the pitch of his voice carried another message—one of foreboding. Poor Dilaver. I felt so sorry for him. He (like everyone else under this group's control) was now powerless to do anything—except travel to Bingol when it was all over and report what had happened. (See map on p. 20.)

The rest began to form up into a little group behind us with their captives. I had the impression, although it was too dark to be sure, that they had taken more prisoners than just the four of us. The fact that everybody was now dressed like guerrillas made it difficult to know who was who. Of course the most disturbing aspect of being dressed like guerrillas was that we were now likely to be shot with them in any future military engagement.

A young man in his late teens took me by the arm. With a quick gesture towards the mountains that loomed darkly above us, he said something that sounded like '*Wheken, Wheken,* Professor,' which I assumed meant 'Let's go, Professor.' I said 'OK,' not stopping to think that 'OK' was one of those non-Kurdish Westernisms that had been banned earlier in the evening—the kind of term George Bush might use. As he led me down into the dry gully, this young man shook his head, and said firmly,

'*Tammum* Professor!'

I was getting my first Kurdish lesson. He repeated the word

tammum adding to it the word *Kurdi,* to show me that *tammum* was the Kurdish word for 'OK'. Not wanting to be thought a slow learner, I made the appropriate response.

'*Tammum,*' I parroted.

My teacher seemed pleased with me, and repeated with quiet satisfaction the words '*Tammum; Kurdi.*'

As we picked our way up the other side of the gully, I couldn't help chuckling inwardly. *Tammum* is not a word used only in Kurdish; it is also used very commonly in Turkey, Saudi Arabia and other Middle Eastern countries. However, rather than be a purist about it, I decided to stay with the word. Besides, he had the gun; so anything he said was *tammum* with me.

As we emerged from that little dry gully, I experienced a curious sense of relief. It was almost as though I were leaving behind there, in that little 'valley of the shadow of death', all those ominous images of my execution.

Immediately we began to stride out. Our captors were obviously in a hurry to reach the cover of the mountains. The young guard walking with me was at the head of a column that strung out behind us in Indian file. After a period of very brisk trekking, we began to move up into the sparsely wooded foothills. There we found ourselves scrambling up slopes covered with dry grass and strewn with black rocky outcrops.

As the steepness increased, we began to lose our footing on this treacherous surface. Because of my 'bargain' saddle boots, I suspected I was probably having more trouble climbing than anyone else. The soles on my boots, unlike the rubber ones on everybody else's footwear, were made of synthetic leather. They are incredibly long-wearing; virtually indestructible, in fact. But on this kind of surface I found they had almost no grip. Matters were even worse; the effect of all the rocks and grass on the soles was most peculiar. It actually smoothed and polished them.

After we'd been walking and climbing for about half an hour, we stopped to rest. I turned to look down the slope and into the valley where I thought the road would be. I could still see a line of stationary headlights. The road-block was obviously still in place and under guard. Doubtless everyone was being detained there to ensure adequate getaway time for us. Even from that distance, I could still hear faintly the sound of voices.

As the rest of the column began to arrive, my guard touched me on the shoulder. Having secured my attention, he pointed to himself and began to use the universal hand-signal method of indicating numbers. He clenched both fists then opened them to indicate the number ten. Then he added five fingers with his right hand and three with his left—a total of eighteen. Then he pointed to himself again.

He was telling me that he was eighteen years old. I nodded to indicate that I had read his silent message correctly.

He pointed his index finger towards me and raised his eye-brows as if to say, 'How old are you, Professor?'

Hoping that his computational skills were equal to the task, I opened and closed my fists five times then added another nine digits.

He nodded his understanding.

The fact that he now knew my age triggered off an irritating little thought in the back of my mind.

'Hope he doesn't think I'm having trouble climbing these slopes because I'm too old.' I was determined not to be cat-egorised, by some Kurdish kid not even a third my age, as an unfit Australian geriatric. So hanging on to a sapling for balance,

I showed him the sole of one of my boots. I rubbed the shiny surface with the palm of my hand. Then lowering my foot I turned uphill and mimed the frictionless downward movement that was causing me so much trouble and frustration.

It was suddenly time to move on. A number of others took the lead this time. We all began to head diagonally upwards around the foothill; a course which would eventually bring us to the side of a vast mountain valley.

I doubted that the valley was our destination. It was far too accessible to our pursuers, who would probably start searching for us from the point on the road where we had been kidnapped. Besides, one does not climb up unnecessary foothills to go down into a valley. They were taking us, I was sure, to some place high on that mountain range. If I was right, I had a long upward journey ahead of me in these wretched boots. The tree-cover became thicker as we gained altitude. I grabbed every sapling tree and branch I could to stop myself from slipping downhill. I must say I was grateful for the assistance of my guard.

When we stopped for our next short break, I looked back over the valley behind us. The vehicle lights were no longer visible, hidden by a low hill, but their reflection could still be dimly seen against the dark mountains beyond.

I looked along the contour of the foothill where we were all now standing regaining our breath. Richard was nearby; Ron and Marvin were some little distance away.

It was then that I noticed a gentleman whom I'd not seen before, standing quite close to me. Since he had no gun, I knew he had to be a hostage. His complexion was dark. His forehead was high and his thick glossy hair was combed straight back over his head and temples. He was of medium height—shorter than I and, I guessed, a few years younger too. He was wearing a *şalvar*, a type of trousers still commonly worn in parts of the Middle East. Most of the guerrillas with us wore tighter fitting modifications of the *şalvar*. The garment in its classic form is very full and floppy both in the seat and around the abdomen. Its crutch is cut very low and hangs in generous folds between the legs. The legs themselves are enormously wide and loose-fitting in comparison to Western trousers. They billow out at the knees, but below have ankle-tight cuffs. For some strange reason I cannot explain,

Gary Thomas

people who wear the *şalvar* without those pointy-toed shoes that curl up at the front never seem fully dressed to me.

As I looked down at the man's feet, I was surprised to see that he was not wearing shoes of any sort. All the poor chap had on was a pair of flimsy sandals.

His foot problem was worse than mine, I was sure. I felt sorry for him and decided to strike up a conversation. I hoped there was a way to do so without giving our guards the impression that we were planning to escape. Since they couldn't understand what we were saying, the way we said it would be all-important. Both volume and tone would have to be just right.

The volume would have to be 'quiet'. Voices carry long distances across mountains like these; especially on still nights like this.

As to tone, 'brash' was definitely out. We were after all prisoners, and anything we said that sounded cocky or angry would not go down too well with some of our more volatile captors. 'Earnest' was also out—it could be too easily interpreted as conspiratorial. I finally decided that 'quietly casual' would be about right.

So trying to sound a bit like a rather laid-back newsreader delivering a boring weather forecast, I initiated my conversation.

'How are you doing?' I asked.

'Oh, not too bad, you know,' he replied, in an unmistakable accent.

'You're Welsh, aren't you?' I asked.

'That's right, I am,' he said with some surprise, 'but I've lived in London for many years.'

'You've retained your accent,' I said. 'Did you come from Cardiff?'

'Good God! How did you know that?' he asked, with the open-mouthed incredulity of a Liza Doolittle.

'Didn't really,' I laughed. 'I guessed. I'm no Professor Higgins. The only Welsh people I know come from Cardiff, and I thought your accent sounded a bit like theirs.'

I proffered my hand. 'I'm Allen Roberts from Australia.'

'Gary Thomas,' he responded.

'How did you come to be caught up in all this, Gary?'

'I haven't the slightest idea,' he replied, as he hunched his shoulders and held his palms upward.

'Were you in that tourist bus?'

'Yes, I was,' he answered. 'I was on my way to Lake Van.' With a rueful smile he added, 'I was going on a holiday.'

Our conversation was abruptly cut short by the order to move on again. As I suspected, we were now heading up along the steep side of that huge valley. This time I was somewhere in the centre of the column. I knew that Gary was not far behind me, but couldn't tell where Marvin, Ron and Richard were.

As far as I could make out at this stage, they'd taken only five of us as hostages: three Americans, one Britisher and one Australian; an interesting selection of nationalities. 'Perhaps they intend using us for bargaining purposes,' I thought as I struggled up the steepening incline. I just couldn't see though how a couple of men engaged in archaeological research, a business consultant, a travel agent and a tourist would be considered valuable currency in any deal with our respective governments. In any case, I told myself, none of our governments would enter into such deals. The US Government policy was certainly clear—no negotiation with terrorists—and I guessed Britain and Australia would take the same stance in respect of Gary and myself.

Maybe they think we're spies!' I thought. (The idea was by no means a wild one. A few years back, precisely that had happened to Ron Wyatt. Someone had informed certain Middle-Eastern authorities that he was a spy. The result was that he and his two sons were thrown into prison and were held there without trial for about three months.)

Maybe we were on our way to some remote mountain prison in Eastern Turkey, or even over the border in Iraq, to become long-term hostages like Jackie Mann and Terry Waite.

The fact that our captors had given us warm clothing and assisted us as we climbed suggested that their plan was not to cause us personal harm—at least not, in the short term. Long-term, who could tell?

For the best part of half an hour, we continued to scramble up through the thick forest cover on the mountainside. As we climbed higher we had to ford a number of small streams which trickled down between the rocks. We paused at one of these just long enough to gulp down a few mouthfuls of water before moving on.

When we stopped again, we were high on the shoulder of the mountain spur which formed one side of that great valley. I estimated that we had climbed about a thousand feet since leaving the road. I looked out to my right through the dark tracery of trees. The mountain bluff at the head of the valley was at least a thousand feet higher than we were.

'How much farther do they intend taking us tonight?' I wondered as I stood there, my knees barely holding me upright, the back of my throat burning and my chest heaving.

I looked back down the mountain. The forest obscured everything. I was certain that the road from which we had been taken would be empty by now anyway. All the vehicles in our convoy would be well on their way to Bingol—if they were not already there.

I was sure that information gained from Dilaver and others would be quickly communicated to the relevant Turkish authorities. Within a day or two at the most, our names and what had happened to us would be in the hands of our respective governments and families.

My wife, Margaret, would be asleep right now. I was sure that the news of our abduction would raise some very disturbing questions for my wife and family—unanswerable questions: Where is he now? Is he alive or dead? What will happen to him and the others with him?

I felt some relief that my wife would not have to bear the burden of these questions for a little while at least. I also took comfort from the thought that all our wives and families would give each other strong personal and prayerful support once the news broke.

As things stood, however, all the normal links between each of us and our families had been broken; sundered by the bizarre events of this night. But there was even more to it than this. Our links with the twentieth century had also been severed.

From the moment we left that road, it was as though we had virtually lost our identity as people of modern Western culture. Whether we liked it or not, we had now been thrust into a culture that was totally alien to ours—a culture already old when ours had barely begun.

My eyes began to trace the undulating line of the ridge on the other side of the awesome black valley. For just a moment, the ridge reminded me of some dark giant wave suddenly thrust up by a powerful undertow, its long uneven crest mounting and quivering before breaking; the threatening steepness and mass of its highest point hovering, hovering before its all-engulfing collapse.

I sensed in that moment that we were all at the mercy of these mountains, and the men who lived in them.

Our capture had taken away not only any initiative we might have exercised over our own lives, but also our control of the important archaeological project that had brought us this summer to Turkey. Begun many years ago, this project had involved us in a great deal of painstaking, costly and at times life-endangering field-work. It had also involved long-term negotiations with the Turkish government.

We had just reached the point where our next step was the critically important preliminary dig. To get the necessary permit, we had been conferring for the last two days in Ankara with high-ranking Turkish Government officials. As a result of our meetings, it now seemed certain that our dig would be under way within ten days.

For both Ron and myself this represented the fulfilment of an almost lifelong dream, that of excavating the Nuh'un Gemisi site, considered by many to be potentially the most significant archaeological site in the world.

Unlike most dreams we mortals dream, this one was right within our grasp. Until tonight, when it was dashed at our feet; perhaps destroyed for ever by a band of young Kurdish guerrillas.

CHAPTER

2

Nuh'un Gemisi

The Nuh'un Gemisi ('the ark of Noah') quest which had brought me to Turkey a number of times, this time to be kidnapped, began for me over thirty years ago.

It all started in 1960 when I came across an article in Australia's *PIX* magazine entitled 'Is this Noah's Ark?'[1] As a young historian with a deep interest in biblical history and archaeology, my curiosity was stirred.

The article described how an American team had journeyed to the mountains of Eastern Turkey to investigate a large mud-covered boat-shaped formation located near the border of Iran. It sat on the mud of a broad valley known by the locals as Akyayla which means 'white high plateau'. It was at an altitude of several thousand feet above sea level and, according to information in the article, its dimensions were similar to those of the ark as set down in the Old Testament.

I was particularly intrigued by some of the on-site photographs published with the article; especially the one on p. 28.

The article also described (again with photographs) how the investigation team had exploded sections of the formation with dynamite to see if there were any wood inside. The absence of such wood apparently confirmed their opinion that this was not the ark but some sort of natural formation.

On the basis of this article, I felt that the site warranted further investigation and developed a secret desire to go there one day and check it personally.

Camera Press from Pix

Little did I realise that across the Pacific in the United States of America, another young man, about my age, had read that same article published in his country by *LIFE* Magazine.

That man was Ron Wyatt. He too had a profound interest in biblical archaeology, and he too cherished a desire to investigate the site for himself.

For a period of several years, however, the formation received little archaeological attention, mainly because of the dangerous political situation and climatic restraints of the region.[2]

Although there was a good deal of ongoing interest in locating the ark during this period, it had not been focused upon the Akyayla site but upon nearby Mount Ararat. It was not until the 1970s and 1980s that systematic research began on the Akyayla boat-shaped object. Early in this period Ron Wyatt went there several times and was one of the first to submit the formation to careful investigation. There is little doubt that it was his persistent work in co-operation with the Turkish authorities and a number of others that led to the site's being recognised as one of archaeological significance.

In the 1980s the Turkish government set up a Prime-Ministerially-authorised project, operating from Ataturk University at Erzurun and also from Los Alamos National Laboratory at the University of California, to investigate the site thoroughly.[3] Much of the research involved in this and other scientific investigations led Sevket Ekinci, Governor of Agri and Chairman of the Noah's Ark Commission, officially to declare the site a national park. The park was solemnly dedicated as the place where the remains of Noah's Ark were believed to exist. Mr Gengiz Cokce, Head Official of the District of Dogubayazit, Mr Osman Baydar, President of the Municipality and many others were present.[4]

The occasion of the ceremony had been well documented by the press both in Turkey and overseas. Film footage of the occasion had been televised in Turkey and the United States. Video tapes including it had been widely distributed in several countries and were still readily available. As official confirmation of the site's recognition, an impressive Visitors' Centre was built overlooking the formation.

My own interest in the formation was rekindled in 1989 when I was given David Fasold's book, *The Discovery of Noah's Ark*.[5] The book told how he had worked with Ron Wyatt to discover whether the structures inside the formation were those of a real boat. David Fasold's background as a qualified ship's master and marine salvage expert enabled him, I thought, to bring valuable insights to bear upon the research data, especially that derived from electronic sub-surface techniques. At this time I felt I had studied the Akyayla site long enough from afar, and so when I received Ron Wyatt's address and some financial encouragement from a friend, I determined to make contact with him. I did this initially by numerous long-distance phone calls, letters and faxes. Ron and his wife Mary Nell also sent me photographs, video tapes, a range of data and copies of Ron's book (*Discovered: Noah's Ark!*)[6] documenting their research up to that point. The information thus gained confirmed my own opinion that the formation needed to be properly and promptly excavated. I therefore resolved to visit the site at the first opportunity.

And so it was finally arranged in late July of 1990 that my wife should fly back to Australia from London where we'd been staying, and I should fly to Turkey. My intention was to meet Ron in the town of Dogubayazit to examine the site with him and then, hopefully, to arrange with the Turkish Government for a preliminary dig, beginning if possible that very summer.

When I arrived in Dogubayazit I discovered that Ron was not there to meet me. He was back home in Nashville. Due to the mounting threat of war with Saddam Hussein, the dig had been put on hold.

Naturally I was disappointed. However, I determined to make the most of the opportunity I now had to examine the formation. Next morning saw me high in the mountains of Ararat and ready with all my equipment to examine the site.

I shall never forget my first view of the formation. In spite of all my research I was not really prepared. There in the valley below was the gigantic 'boat' with pointed 'prow' and rounded 'stern', symmetrical too and as big as a battleship.

The mud-covered boat-shaped formation (*Turkish Mapping Service: Camera Press from* Pix)

And here I was, about to complete the last half-mile of a journey which had begun in my mind thirty years ago and had brought me half-way around the world to this place and to this moment.

For the next week, I carried out the most complete examination of the formation and its environs that I could manage. This involved a comprehensive photographic survey and an on-site study of structures, rocks and soils. Various measurements were also taken.

By the time I was ready to leave, I felt that probably sufficient data now existed to justify a strong case for the site to be thoroughly excavated. This data had not been amassed haphazardly.

It was the result of a long and careful process, to which many people had contributed. Several like myself had made a feature-by-feature comparison of what the Old Testament record said about Noah's ark, with what had been found on this site.

Although no one had yet had opportunity to do a proper excavation of the formation, there certainly seemed to be enough evidence available to warrant one.

As a historian, I had long believed that archaeology was in many respects like detective work. The method used is very similar, especially if one compares it with the detective's approach to finding and identifying a missing person.

The detective begins by questioning those who knew the missing person, to get a detailed description. He also questions those who have information about where the person was last seen and, if possible, the circumstances leading to his disappearance. From all of this the detective is able to make a check-list on the basis of which he initiates an informed search.

This approach was used during the nineteenth century by Heinrich Schliemann who sensed that Homer's account of Troy—its siege, the wooden horse and other events described there—had the marks of an eye-witness account that could be historically accurate. Although experts disagreed with him, Schliemann attempted to locate Troy using the clues on his check-list. The rest is archaeological history. Schliemann discovered Troy; and although his pioneering techniques are not all to be emulated, his check-list approach is a good one and is still used by archaeological researchers.

This approach would appear to be appropriate for those engaged in a search for an ancient vessel such as Noah's ark. One does not begin with the *a priori* assumption that there is no such thing as an ark and therefore not bother to look. Had Schliemann reasoned this way, he would not have discovered Troy. One should begin, no matter what one believes, by taking the record, assuming that it *could* be true, and then testing its features in the field.

Those who had searched for the ark on snow-covered Mount Ararat had generally assumed that although it would now be thousands of years old, it might be preserved there under the ice, as for example ancient mammoths have been preserved in Siberia. However, since the formation of the Akyayla site was below the snow line, it would seem reasonable to assume that the ark, if it were there, would have had to be preserved in some other way—possibly by a process of petrification, which, contrary to popular belief, can and does occur quite rapidly. This fact is clearly evidenced, for example, by the petrification of the wooden piles supporting the buildings of Venice.[7]

If he is searching for an ancient vessel such as Noah's ark, the historian engaged in archaeological research begins by carefully examining the historical records of the time and from them constructs his check-list. He then goes into the field and using this check-list compares, point for point, what is on it with what he finds. The more features that correspond, the more likely it is that he has found what he is looking for. This entire process should involve a willingness to examine all the forthcoming evidence, while maintaining throughout the process a reasonable open-mindedness and healthy scepticism.

Anyone who examines ancient anthropological literature will find that the account of a world-wide flood and a Noah-like character, who with his family and a host of animals was saved in a great boat, is one of the commonest of accounts. Most nations seem to have it in some recognisable form or other in their folklore. A. M. Rehwinkel, along with others, cites numerous examples from around the world. In his book *The Flood*[8] he presents many of these. One for example from Alaska tells how the father of the Indian tribe lived toward the rising sun.

> Having been warned in a dream that a deluge would devastate the earth, he built a raft, on which he saved himself, his family and all the animals. He floated several months on the water. The animals, who could then talk, complained and murmured against him. A new earth at length appeared. He therefore alighted with all the animals which then lost the gift of speech as punishment for their complaining.

The Koran (notably in Chapter XI) provides quite a full account of Noah, the ark and the flood.[9] Perhaps the best-known extra-biblical flood account is the *Epic of Gilgamesh*[10], a well-developed form of the flood tradition containing many of the features found in Genesis.

It is however in the Genesis account that one finds not only the elements of this basic narrative but the most impressive detail; ideal for an archaeological check-list.

When it comes, for example, to the nature of the ark, its specifications and so on, we are able to note in our check-list its actual dimensions in ancient measurements that can be quite accurately interpreted.[11] Other details are also available. We know for example that it had three decks[12], rooms[13], a kind of window[14] and a door[15]. We know also something about the range of its occupants, human and non-human. All of these details furnish our check-list with a wealth of information about *what* we are seeking.

Concerning *where*, the Genesis account simply states that the ark rested on the mountains of Ararat.[16]

These *what* and *where* check-list criteria had been used by the majority of those engaged in this research to date, and using them as a yardstick it had already been possible to tick off several of them in the field.

Concerning the *what* criteria, this colossal boat-shaped object with its pointed 'prow', its rounded 'stern', its largely symmetrical shape and its 'list to starboard', certainly looked as though it might be a boat—perhaps the ark.

However the possibility of its being the ark was based on far more than appearances. Our check-list from the Old Testament gave a length of 300 cubits, a breadth of 50 cubits and height of 30 cubits.[17] These are very specific measurements. Obviously, to check them out in the field we would need to know the length of the cubit. This is not quite as straightforward as it seems. There were a number of cubit lengths. The 18-inch cubit is the one of which most people are aware. However there is also a 20.6-inch cubit which is not quite so well known.

From the evidence of several researchers, including Piazzi Smyth, Scotland's Astronomer Royal in the nineteenth century, there was, I believed, a compelling case for the 20.6-inch cubit as the one most appropriate to the cubit dimensions of the ark.[18] On the basis of a 20.6-inch cubit, the length of the ark would be around 515 ft.

The formation when carefully measured was in fact this length—515 ft.[19]

The width, according to our Old Testament check-list, ought

to have been 86 ft. However, the breadth of the formation when measured was much wider, about 138 ft.[20]

Reasons had been put forward to explain the fact that the formation is so much wider than that set down in the Genesis account. It had been suggested by Ron Wyatt[21] that this might have been the result of 'splaying' due to the fact that, before the 1948 earthquake, the formation had been buried under a huge overburden of mud. However, because the outline of the 'hull' was so sharp and regular (especially as it appeared in the early aerial photograph below) the possibility had been raised that the

Early aerial view of the formation (*Reproduced by permission of Camera Press*)

shape had not been distorted at all. Fasold had held to this view, and had suggested that the breadth of 50 cubits set down in Scripture was not meant to be taken as straight gunwale-to-gunwale width but as an average.[22] He had also maintained that the formation is the remains of a reed boat rather than a wooden one.[23]

These questions concerning the composition and dimensions of the formation were very important ones. However, the ultimate answers would be forthcoming only as result of a dig.

Whether the formation had the right appearance and size to be the ark was not the crucial issue. A natural formation could be of similar appearance and size.[24] The issue of whether it was the ark or not rested upon the question of whether or not there was a boat under that mud covering.

A number of very careful scientific investigations had already yielded enough anomalous data to suggest that the formation might not be natural, but a man-made object—possibly a boat. These investigations had yielded information which, although by no means complete, appeared to be significant and warranted a dig.

For example, using metal-detector scans, some particularly interesting subsurface readings from inside the boat-shaped formation had been gained. These were especially intriguing because there were no such readings outside it.

The first metal-detector investigation was carried out in June 1985 by a team consisting of Ron Wyatt, David Fasold and geologist Dr John Baumgardner[25]—who was later to work with the Turkish/US Project team formed officially to investigate the formation.[26] All three men published details of this work.[27] The detector indicated lines of metal underground. These were found to be in an organised pattern with longitudinal as well as transverse lines. The longitudinal lines converged to points at either end of the site. Dr Baumgardner surmised that the lines represent rows of nails or spikes.[28]

Another metal-detector scan was carried out a few months later and once again, according to Dr Baumgardner, this 're-sulted in the amazing pattern of lines'.[29] The presence of such regular patterns was, of course, strongly indicative that below the surface of the formation was a man-made structure of some kind.[30] That these pieces of metal might be joining mechanisms of the sort one might expect to find in a large boat seemed to be a reasonable possibility. The team were impressed by the fact that the lines were distorted and bunched up as if on impact where the rock outcrop juts into the formation. Dr Baumgardner made particular reference to this in one of his newsletters.[31]

This metal-detector evidence was rated very highly by all those involved in the work. Dr Baumgardner, indeed, gave as his professional opinion that 'the grid of metal lines almost certainly demands that the site contains a man-made structure.'[32]

As one who has done some amateur metal-detecting in the early goldfields of New South Wales and Victoria, I agreed that

Schematic representation of pattern of 'iron lines' (superimposed on author's photograph and drawing on R. Wyatt's field survey photograph)

Schematic representation of pattern of 'iron lines' disrupted by intruding rock (superimposed on author's photograph and drawing on R. Wyatt's field survey photograph)

this metal detection work was significant, especially since it had been carried out and confirmed in the presence of a number of responsible personnel.[33] It had been well documented too.[34] Grid patterns had been marked carefully by long coloured tapes, and much of the process had been both photographed and video-taped. On the basis of this evidence alone, it was clear that the site needed to be excavated.

During the month of July 1987 a joint research project sponsored by Dr H. Ertugrul, Director of Ataturk University, was conducted. Leaders of the research team were M. Salih Bayraktutan of Ataturk University and John R. Baumgardner of the University of California.[35] Other members of the team included Thomas T. Anderson; Maylon T. Wilson of the University of California; Thomas F. Fenner, with Geophysical Survey Systems, Inc, manufacturer of the radar; and Semsi Yazici and Necmettin Tamas of Ataturk University. In addition, James A. Burroughs, Daniel M. Devaney and Jeffrey C. Wayman of Seven League Productions provided photographic documentation for the project.[36] It was the responsibility of this team to carry out a subsurface geophysical survey of the site using ground-penetrating radar, a high-precision magnetometer survey and limited investigations with a one-channel seismograph.[37] The results of these tests were published in a scientific report by Dr John Baumgardner (University of California, Los Alamos National Laboratory) and Dr M. Salih Bayraktutan (Ataturk University, Faculty of Engineering), in November 1987, Erzurum, Turkey.[38]

Once again the results were highly interesting. Concerning the radar scan, this Turkish-Government-sponsored report stated that between four and eight metres below the ground surface there is an almost planar surface which covers a large portion of the site.[39] What is this large flat surface? Dr Baumgardner cautiously suggested in his official letter (15 September 1987) that although he could not provide a definitive answer, there seemed to be two possibilities.

'One,' he wrote, 'is that the surface represents the petrified remains of one of the decks of the Ark, probably the middle deck. The other is that the surface is the flat top of a large boat-shaped piece of bedrock whose dimensions by coincidence happen to match closely those given for the Ark in Genesis.'[40] Whilst cautiously stating in his newsletter that the surface could be bedrock, Dr Baumgardner nonetheless set down in the official university project report two considerations that suggest it is not. The first was that the radar results did not indicate that the surface is similar in nature to the calc-schist rock that forms the adjacent hills on either side of the mudflow and the outcrop of rock that appears to intrude into the formation. The second was that there was a 'double reflection' suggestive of a layer, rather than a simple transition into a material many metres thick; and to find such a layer in this context was highly anomalous from the standpoint of known landslide and debris flow. Dr Baumgardner and Dr Bayraktutan therefore suggested in their official joint report that if the layer pertained to a buoyant man-made structure, its setting suggested that it was transported by a landslide to its present position where it was stranded on the outcropping rock on the middle of the site.[41]

Neither the magnetometer nor the seismographic data were inconsistent with the radar evidence which indicated a large planar surface.[42] The seismograph data in fact, though very limited, revealed the presence of similar material to that indicated by the radar and within similar depth parameters.[43]

The conclusions of this official report affirmed that, 'We conclude that the data from our geophysical investigations in no way conflict with the proposition that the unusual boat-shaped site near Mahser village[44] contains the remains of Noah's ark.' This report, conducted by highly skilled professionals from two countries, went on to add, 'Indeed, the existence of the remains of a large man-made structure in the site is an attractive way to account for the highly anomalous feature of the extensive, almost planar reflector observed in the radar data.'[45] Clearly the fact that there were such anomalous data yielded by these subsurface techniques suggested that there was a distinct possibility that the formation was not a natural one. To clarify the matter, it was recommended that what was needed was actual material, removed from inside, as is stated in the conclusions of the commissioned report:

Without actual samples of the subsurface materials we feel that definitive interpretations of our data are not possible. On the other hand, we believe samples obtainable through core drilling a small number of holes in the site can provide

the information required which, together with the geophysical data we already have, could allow very solid conclusions
to be reached. We therefore urge the Turkish authorities to
support efforts to conduct core drilling as early as 1988, as
weather conditions allow.[46]

It was also recommended 'that core drilling at several locations both inside and outside the site be performed to provide the
additional information needed to make proper interpretations of
these geophysical tests.'[47]

To find and identify this 'almost planar surface'[48], the nature
of these core drillings and the way in which they were to be done
were set down very specifically in recommendations by Drs
Baumgardner and Bayraktutan in the official report and by Dr
Baumgardner in his official newsletters.

In the first place, as Drs Baumgardner and Bayraktutan
stated, drills would need to be sent down 'at several locations'[49]—a wise recommendation, since the formation covers
such a large area. Furthermore the subsurface layers, whatever
they were made of, could well have been fractured, dislocated and
even separated from one another by earthquake activity.

Secondly, the drills would need to be sunk not only within the
formation but outside it as well.[50] In this way, characteristics of
the normal terrain could be ascertained and valid comparisons
made between it and what was inside the perimeters of the
formation.

Thirdly, the drills would need to be sunk to a depth sufficient
not only to locate the planar reflector surface as indicated by the
radar and other survey techniques,[51] but also to reveal important
contextual features, both above and below that surface. Dr
Baumgardner in his official report recommended very appropriately that continuous core sampling be carried out to a depth of
20 m (approximately 65 ft).[52]

Plans were therefore made to carry out this core drilling programme. By 15 September 1987, Dr Baumgardner was able to
report that Dr Bayraktutan had located suitable drilling equipment[53] with the aim of using it on the site in the autumn of that
year.[54]

Dr Baumgardner also reported that permission had been given

by government officials to have the drilling carried out by a special team from Erzurum.

The work was done between 28 July and 7 August[55] but unfortunately, when the drilling was done none of these three recommendations was followed.

A total of only four drill holes was sunk, which in view of the situation was simply not enough; a fact acknowledged by Dr Baumgardner himself when he referred to the severe limitations imposed by such sparseness of core drillings.[56]

Furthermore, no drillings were done outside the formation, to enable the essential geological comparisons to be made. In addition to this, the recommended depth requirement was not met. Consequently, it was not surprising that this critically important planar radar reflector was not encountered, as Dr Baumgardner himself also indicated.[57]

Dr Baumgardner also commented in one of his newsletters concerning the absence of other core-drill evidence, namely, wood,[58] pointing out however that 'Core drilling is severely limited in its ability to find buried archaeological structure especially if it is sparsely distributed and has been significantly altered by decay and chemical weathering'[59]—a situation that would appear in fact to have obtained on this site. Dr Baumgardner was careful to add that the absence of such evidence did not rule out the possibility of the formation's being a man-made object, perhaps the ark:

> We still cannot rule out the scenario that the ark of Noah had landed previously higher on the slope and during the mud slide event was swept downslope and caught on this ridge-shaped island of basement rock.[60]

It seemed abundantly clear to me that what was needed to clarify the matter, perhaps as a first step, was a considerably increased number of core drillings which would penetrate deeply into many areas, not only along the centre line, but also between it and the periphery of the formation, as well as at a number of places along that periphery, some of them perhaps horizontal rather than vertical; this programme also to include many drillings at numerous points outside the formation for control purposes.

The second and ultimate step would be the one recommended by Dr Baumgardner when he said in 1987, '...it appears that we have exhausted the methods available that involve minimal disturbance to the site. The only procedure that makes sense at this juncture, if the critical question of archaeological structure is to be resolved, is to dig.'[61] By 1989 such a dig had not yet been completed. However, because the Turkish Government was holding so much significant information from so many sources, I was certain that eventually a dig would be necessary, and would be initiated.

In spite of its lack of success in locating the planar surface, the core-drilling programme did uncover some other things of considerable significance.

Three of the four drill-hole locations revealed what Dr Baumgardner in the same letter described as 'nodules of bright yellow mineral limonite'.[62] In this setting, it seemed to him anomalous,[63] since he had not observed such limonite previously in 'fissures or exposures in the mudflow clay'.[64] He went on to write in his letter that because of earlier indications that there might be 'unusual amounts of iron in the site', he thought that its occurrence 'could represent the rusted remains of metallic iron objects'.[65] These limonite occurrences were reminiscent of the rusted metal nodules located at Sutton Hoo, where the remains of an Anglo-Saxon ship had been unearthed, about 60 miles north-east of London, England.[66]

The columnar shapes on sections of the exterior walls of the formation (especially those of the north-west and south-east faces) had evoked considerable interest among many who had observed them. On the south-east section, near the southern end of the formation, there were deep slits between these bulging column shapes. The mud veneer which covered them was in places stained a rusty brown colour. Below this thin layer of mud one could see some unusual structures. They appeared to be columns of rock, upright and more or less evenly spaced. The regular spacing of these uprights and their fairly uniform widths had suggested the possibility that they might indeed be ribs—as Ron Wyatt had earlier suggested they were.[67]

Some thorough archaeological work was needed to ascertain what these rib-like structures really were.[68] To determine this

Outlines of perpendicular 'rib' columns visible beneath mud of eastern wall
By permission of Monsieur Rene Haran, Paris, France

Perpendicular mud-covered 'rib' columns on western wall
By permission of Monsieur Rene Haran, Paris, France

would of course require careful excavation, to reveal these structures fully from both outside and inside the formation, along with
careful sampling and analysis to identify precisely their nature
and composition.

All these anomalous features associated with the general
nature and structure of the formation raised some very important
questions. And these questions could not be properly answered
without further investigation and research—ideally, in conjunc-
tion with an excavation.

There were other questions too, many of which arose from the
discovery of various objects on or around the site. While many of
these objects still required further analysis, they were nonetheless
potentially important, in that they opened up leads which needed
to be explored. One was a sample which had the appearance of a
rivet head surrounded by a washer. It was found by Ron Wyatt at
a point just outside the western perimeter of the formation on 23
June 1991. The find was witnessed and fully documented in
writing and signed by some eleven persons.[69]

As a first step, three separate tests were completed on this
sample.[70]

'Metal rivet'

Other samples from the site which occasioned a great deal of interest were those that had been identified as petrified wood. The first of these was found in August 1984 at the northern end of the site where the rounded end of the formation is fretting away and crumbling.[71] This sample had not only the appearance of fossilised wood but gave the impression of having been hand-tooled to produce what was possibly the shoulder of a tenon joint.[72] (See top photo, p. 46.)

The second sample had been removed from the inside of the formation in 1987 by special arrangement with His Excellency Sevket Ekinci, the Governor of Agri, who was present with several other Turkish officials on the site when it was officially declared a National Park. The object, a heavy dark brown rectangular slab of stone, was layered and appeared to have been hand-tooled. Its features had prompted the notion that it might be a piece of laminated 'deck' timber.[73] (Bottom photo, p. 45.)

In the summer of 1990 I was accompanied to the site by Dr G. Smars and Mr J. Bouma who offered to assist me in my research there.[74] Consequently on this occasion I was privileged (as leader of this small team) to be present for the discovery of a black tarry substance which appeared to have oozed out of a possible 'deck support' on the eastern edge of the formation. A small sample of this substance which was first noted by Mr J. Bouma[75] was later identified as bitumen or pitch[76], which is of course specifically mentioned in Genesis 6:14.

Samples of rock-like material found on site had also evoked considerable interest. As result of a number of analyses and because of their general appearance, they had been identified as possibly a form of slag that could have been poured off from a furnace.[77]

In addition to these objects, some interesting samples suggesting the presence of animals had been located. These included antler fragments[78] taken from the formation, several coprolites (egg-shaped pieces of animal dung[79]) and numerous strands of animal hair from inside the western wall of the formation.[80]

Then there were the large stones discovered across the valley. They resembled drogue stones, used in the ancient world to steer or anchor vessels. Although drogue stones are not uncommon artefacts,[81] none of those which had been found seemed to be

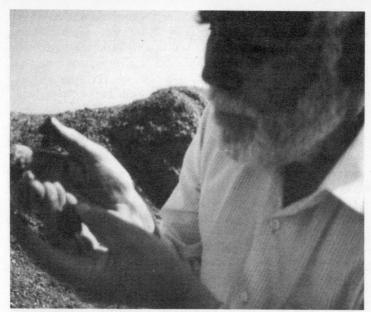

Pitch-like material found on site

Stone slab of 'petrified deck timber'

'Hand-tooled' shoulder of 'tenon joint'

anywhere near the size of the ones found near the village of Arzap which was within visual distance of the Akyayla site. The stones in this area were up to ten feet high and weighed several tons. A dozen or so of them had been found in the region where the boat-shaped formation lay. Like other drogue stones, their holes had been carefully hollowed out and designed to receive knotted ropes. It had been suggested that if these gigantic stones had been attached to a vessel such as the ark, they could well have served as sheet anchors to direct it and prevent it from broaching in the heavy seas of a cataclysmic flood.

This evidence, though somewhat fragmentary and requiring further confirmation, seemed cumulatively to strengthen the possibility that *what* was here, under the mud, was quite possibly a gigantic man-made structure—a boat, in fact.

Concerning the ark's location—the *where* factor—the formation appeared to check out very well. The range of mountains on which the formation presently rested could quite legitimately be termed the mountains of Ararat, or the Ararat mountain range. Ararat is the modern name for Urartu, an ancient kingdom which included this very range of mountains.[82]

Also on the matter of location, our Old Testament checklist indicated that the ark rested 'on' the mountains—that is, at some

Petrified 'deer antler tip' from mud of western wall of the formation
A. S. Roberts

Possible 'slag' found at the site
Ron Wyatt

Coprolite (petrified animal dung)

'Drogue stone' at Arzap

elevation.[83] The formation is in fact at an altitude of about 6,300 feet above sea level.

In addition to this Genesis information, there were other clues that indicated where the ark rested. Flavius Josephus, the Jewish historian who wrote in the first century AD, claimed that all writers of barbarian histories make mention of the flood. Then concerning its resting place Josephus went on to cite Berosus, who lived in the third century BC. Josephus quotes him thus:

> It is said there is still some part of this ship in Armenia at the mountain of the Cordyaeans and that some people carry off pieces of the bitumen which they take away and use chiefly as amulets for the averting of mischiefs.[84]

The name 'Cordyaeans' would appear to refer to those who inhabited this region.[85] The Koran states that the ark came to rest upon Al Judi.[86] To this day, the locals call the mountain on that part of the range where the formation rests Al Judi.[87]

Several ancient names still extant in the near vicinity of the formation have echoes of the flood account in Genesis. For example there is a nearby village called Kargaconmaz, which means 'crow will not stand'; another is called 'The Village of the Eight'[88]. While any of these names might not confirm the site, several of them (which do in fact exist) begin to assume more significance when considered cumulatively.

The area where the formation now rested did not seem to be at odds with major historical references to the ark's resting place.

Before leaving Turkey, I discussed possible future arrangements with Ron by phone. We both agreed that we should begin preparations for a preliminary dig in the following summer. This would involve recording, professionally documenting and marshalling our data so that it could be presented to embassies, government officials and a range of others whose assistance would be sought.[89]

On my return to Australia, I began to do this. I went on to share data from the site with colleagues and friends. Interest grew so rapidly that an old friend, John McNicol, suggested that a research association be formed to encourage and support the work as an Australian initiative. This was done early in 1991.

Well before the summer of 1991, Ron and I had completed

arrangements for our next trip to Turkey. Our aim for this trip was twofold: to complete some more field work on and near the Akyayla site, and to meet with Turkish Government Ministers and others to secure a preliminary dig permit, if possible for that same summer.

We went to Turkey as planned and completed our field work on the site. However, we did not get our important meeting. Since there was no purpose in remaining in Turkey, Ron decided to return to America and I to England. The plan was that I would wait in England until the Turkish official arranging our meeting contacted me. I would then phone Ron in Nashville, Tennessee, and we would both fly to Ankara where, hopefully, we would have our meeting and receive our permit. We estimated that the preliminary dig could be completed in four to six weeks, before winter began.

And so we both waited. Ron continued his normal work as an anaesthetist in a Nashville hospital, while I worked on a book I was writing. I also took the opportunity to do some fossil-fossicking in the gravel pits of Wiltshire.

Weeks passed. A month was soon gone. My progressively extended stay with my old friends Arthur and Vivienne Roderick and their family became a standing joke. Throughout this time I kept in continuous contact with Ankara through the Turkish Embassy in London. As the period lengthened to almost two months, I realised that this unresolved situation could not continue much longer. I was just about to make plans to return home when I received a phone call from the Turkish Ambassador's Secretary in London.

He began his phone call by saying he had some bad news for me. The Turkish gentleman who had been organising the meeting, and ultimately the issuing of our permit to dig, had just been tragically killed in Ankara. He told me that this important man's demise would seriously affect arrangements for our meeting and the issue of our permit. He advised me to defer our plans and arrangements until the summer of the following year. Regretfully, on this advice I made reservations to fly home to Australia the next day. I phoned Ron, who agreed this was our only option.

I was just about to pack my bags when I received another call from the Turkish Embassy. This time they told me that they had just received good news. Word had come from Ankara that our meeting had been set for the Thursday of the following week. I cancelled my reservation to Australia, notified my wife and then phoned Ron. We agreed to fly to Ankara for our meeting on Wednesday 28 August 1991.

How pleased I was on the morning of that day in Ankara to meet Ron, as well as Richard and Marvin who had both accompanied him from America! And how wonderful it was, after waiting so long for this vital meeting, to be told later that day by the man behind the desk at Parliament House that a committee of high-ranking officials from the Turkish Ministry of Culture were ready right then to meet us.

The meeting went very well. We were welcomed most cordially and our proposals for the protection and development of the site were considered and discussed very warmly and thoughtfully. The Director of Excavations for Turkey, who was present at the meeting, had already examined the Akyayla formation and well understood the need for prompt action concerning it.

Before the meeting was over, arrangements had been made for us to go the following day to the Department of Foreign Affairs who would organise the permit to dig.

Next morning we attended this meeting to discuss the project and the granting of our permit. Again the officials in this meeting were most positive about the whole project which we all discussed with enthusiasm as we sipped our *çay*, the Turkish tea which one drinks from tiny glass cups. It was quite certain from our conversation that they had no objection to the granting of our permit. But there would be a delay of some ten days, they thought, before it would be officially issued to us, due to the fact that Turkey was about to enter one of its Muslim religious observance periods.

We were of course delighted with this positive response. We returned to our hotel to discuss plans, not only for the dig but for the ensuing ten-day period prior to receipt of our written permission. We eventually decided to utilise this short delay by travelling to the Nemrut Dag area in the South-East to complete some investigations already begun; and perhaps then to fly to Israel to further some additional work near the Dead Sea.

On the basis of these arrangements we flew to Erzurum, planning to travel by road from there to Bingol and thence to Nemrut Dag. By Friday afternoon the four of us were all loaded up and ready to begin our minibus trip to Bingol. Dilaver our trusted guide and old friend had organised both the vehicle and its driver.

I faxed a brief note to my wife in Australia telling her that at last things had begun to move very rapidly and that we were greatly encouraged by developments. I also gave her some time parameters. I estimated that if we started the preliminary dig in about two weeks, we might finish about five or six weeks later.

I had been away for about three months, and although I longed to return home I was determined (as all four of us were now) to complete the job. In this vein I wrote the following words to my wife: 'As much as I am keen to come home, it is perfectly clear that the project must proceed as quickly as possible...'.[90]

I was so pleased after months of frustrating uncertainty and delay to tell my wife that at last we had made some plans that would not be wrecked by unforeseen circumstances.

Who could have believed that before midnight on this very day, we would all be scrambling at gunpoint half-way up the precipitous side of what the locals call 'Black Hell Valley'?

NOTES

1. Australian *PIX* magazine of July 1960. This was by no means the earliest press report of the boat-shaped formation which appeared following an earthquake some time in 1948. It was photographed during an aerial survey and subsequently commented upon by Capt Ilhan Durupinar, an officer in the Turkish Armed Forces. Long before this a newspaper article headed 'We have seen Noah's Ark...but not on Mount Ararat' was published in *France-Soir*, 31 August 1949. Although written in a jocular style, the article is nonetheless significant historically, since it indicates that two Turkish journalists had visited the area and given location and dimension details which have been confirmed by subsequent investigation as reasonably accurate. The article gives the location as 'Al Judi on the Mesopotamian border' and describes the object as a vessel 500 ft long, 80 ft wide and 50 ft high. This report establishes that the site was known and reported in the press as a possible ark location in the year following what appears to be its initial appearance in 1948—some ten years before Durupinar is said to have identified it in 1959. André Parrot, Curator-in-Chief of the French National Museums and Professor of the Ecole du Louvre, made reference to this Turkish newspaper report in his *Déluge et Arche de Noé*, Delachaux et Niestle, Neuchâtel 1953, which was translated from the French by Edwin Hudson and first published in its English edition by Camelot Press Ltd, London and Southampton in 1955.

2. The formation rests just under 6,300 ft elevation at 44° 15'E and 39° 26'N, as indicated on map ONC G-4 12 and further confirmed on page 3 of the Official Report of the July 1987 Geophysical Investigation of Noah's Ark (Durupinar Site). It is about ten miles (16 km) ESE of Dogubayazit in the province of Agri, and is adjacent to the village of Mahser. Mount Ararat is across the valley approximately 17 miles to the north of the site. The area where it is found has been politically unstable, and often dangerous, bordering as it does nearby former Soviet Russia to the north, Iran immediately to the east and Iraq to the south. Access to the region is also difficult because it is under snow for about eight months of each year.

3. This official November 1987 Report from Ezurum, Turkey was entitled

> JULY 1987 GEOPHYSICAL INVESTIGATION
> OF NOAH'S ARK (DURUPINAR SITE)
> MAHSER VILLAGE DOGUBAYAZIT, AGRI

The report states on page 2 that these two university project teams were operating with the authorisation of the Turkish Prime Minister. On the final page (49) of the same report, thanks are expressed to Professor Dr Hursit Ertugrul, Rector of Ataturk University, for sponsoring the project, to Mr Rüsdu Naiboglu (Emeritus General) Director of Security Affairs and to the Turkish Prime Ministry and Governor of Agri, thanks for their sincere efforts and assistance in making the project a success.

4. Hurriyet 21 Harizan (June) 1987, article entitled 'NUH'UN GEMISI turizme acildi' ('Noah's Ark opening to tourism').

In 1991 along with Ron Wyatt, Richard Rives and Marvin Wilson, the author personally discussed (in Ankara, just two days prior to his kidnapping) with Foreign Affairs Minister, Mr Mehemet Yilmaz, and his colleagues, matters associated with excavating, protecting and developing this registered archaeological site. The author also discussed the same matters a number of times in Erzurum, then later by phone, with Dr Salih Bayraktutan, leader of the joint university research project and member of the Noah's Ark Commission.

5. D. Fasold, *The Ark of Noah* (Wynwood Press: New York, NY), 1988.

6. R. Wyatt, *Discovered: Noah's Ark!* (World Bible Society: Nashville, TN), 1989.

7. Viscount Norwich, Chairman of 'Venice in Peril', the British Committee for the Preservation of Venice, paper, Royal Institution *Proceedings*, May 1991, pp 250-251. Concerning the threat of subsidence and the wooden piles beneath the Companille of St Mark which was begun possibly as early as 888 AD and certainly not later than 912 AD, Viscount Lord Norwich describes what the engineers found when given an 'unprecedented opportunity to examine the complete extent of the foundations of what was one of the oldest buildings in the city...': 'There were the original piles, not as tightly packed

as they would have been later and still in remarkably good condition. It was not thanks to them that the tower had fallen. These Venetian piles, driven deep into the lagoon mud where they had no contact with the air, within a relatively short space of time became petrified, as tough as the rock of Manhattan island—so tough indeed, that during the resto ation a few years ago of the Church of the Gesuiti, one of them actually broke the steel bit of the modern drilling equipment.' This well-documented information establishes the fact that petrification of these wooden logs occurred within a period of no more than about 1,100 years. There is a variety of petrification processes, three of which are:

(i)   atom-by-atom silica replacement;
(ii) migration of metallic ions; and,
(iii) percolation through porous material of carbonate-rich fluids.

The examples hereunder are not cited to demonstrate the process by which petrification might have occurred at the Akyayla site, but simply to illustrate the rapidity with which the process can occur.

The Clermont Ferrands Petrifying Fountains in central France are famous, containing astonified wood, animals, including snakes and birds. (See *The Story of The World In Pictures*, ed Harley Usill BA and H. Douglas Thompson MA, Oldhams: London 1934, p. 12. The picture published clearly shows that all of these objects have been posed in tableau before the petrification process began.) A similar process appears to have occurred in England, at the Mother Shipton's Cave and Petrifying Well at Knaresborough, North Yorkshire. (See Allan Pentecost, 'Springs That Turn Life To Stone', *New Scientist*, 21/28 December 1991, an article made available by Pentecost when researching travertine at King's College, London, for use by Mr Robert McBratney, manager of Mother Shipton's Cave which is featured in the article.) A range of objects demonstrates a similar process which occurs at this site in a matter of months. The author (of this present work) has two artefacts from there, one a moccasin and the other a child's toy rabbit. The possibility therefore that a boat, if it were made of wood, could have been preserved by some petrification process in the course of 4,000-5,000 years (the possible age of the ark according to certain Old Testament chronologies) is by no means an unreasonable one. Whether the formation at the Akyayla site was made of wood or something else—perhaps reeds, as David Fasold (along with some other researchers) suggests—can be determined conclusively only by excavation and careful scientific analysis.

8. A.M. Rehwinkel, *The Flood* (Concordia Publishing House: St Louis, MO, 1951).

9. *The Koran with explanatory notes* (Charles Daly: London, 1832), ch XI.

10. *The Epic of Gilgamesh* (Penguin: Mitcham, Victoria, 1960).

11. Gen 6:15,16 (KJV).

12. Gen 6:16 (KJV).

13. Gen 6:14 (KJV).

14. Gen 6:16 (KJV).

15. Ibid.

16. Gen 8:4 (KJV).

17. Gen 6:15 (KJV).

18. Piazzi-Smyth, *The Great Pyramid* (Bell Publishing Co: New York, NY, 1978), ch XVI, pp 331-353. Piazzi-Smyth, by gathering data from the Great Pyramid and also from a wide range of ancient cubit measures employed by Middle-Eastern and Mediterranean countries, postulated a very precise length for the cubit of 20.68 inches. Further confirmation of an approximately 20.6-inch cubit is found in Nancy Jenkins' *The Boat Beneath the Pyramid* (Holt, Rinehart and Winston, New York, NY, 1980), p 68, where the author states, on the authority of her Special Consultant and Custodian of the Vessel Ahmed Youssef Moustafa, that the old Egyptian cubit was the equivalent of 52.3 cm, which is approximately 20.6 inches. It is strange that in view of the fact that there is such a cubit (and indeed another one of around 22 inches— 56 cms) as has been confirmed by Meir Ben-Dov in his excavational work at Jerusalem (see his *In the Shadow of the Temple, The discovery of Ancient Jerusalem*, Harper and Row: London, 1985, p 142), that many researchers have not seriously considered any cubit other than the 18-inch one. It is also unfortunate that this tendency has resulted in at least one English Bible translation, the New International Version, giving (on the basis of an 18-inch cubit) the length of the ark as 450 ft. The measure cited in the book of Genesis is the cubit, not the foot, and this fact together with the assumption that the cubit is 18 inches makes such a rendering an interpretation rather than a translation.

19. The length of 515 ft is confirmed by measurements taken by Maylon Wilson and Dr John Baumgardner in August 1985 using sophisticated equipment (see R. Wyatt, *Discovered: Noah's Ark!*, p 14, and also David Fasold, *The Ark of Noah*, p 126). Fasold raises the possibility that a 'bow extension' which he has observed would make the overall length approximately 531 ft (ibid, p 127).

20. This measurement has also been confirmed by the personnel mentioned in note 19.

21. R. Wyatt, *Discovered: Noah's Ark!*, p 25, has included a diagram to show how, under pressure from the overburden of mud, an original width of 85.9 ft might well have been increased to 138 ft, its current breadth.

22. D. Fasold, *The Ark of Noah*, in his chapter on Field Surveys (p 115 ff), uses field measurements to present a mathematical thesis involving pi and the golden mean or section, justifying the width of approximately 138 ft. In his

56 *Arksearch*

March/April *Ark-Update* (Noahide Society, Poway, California, p 20), Fasold writes that the formation is 6,180 inches in length or 300 cubits and that marine engineers calculate the area within this formation divided by the length would be 1,027.57 inches for an average width of 49.88 cubits. Marine engineer Samuel R. Windsor has submitted an article dealing with the Akyayla formation to *Catastrophism and Ancient History*, entitled 'Noah's Vessel 24,000 Deadweight Tons'. It was published in Volume XIV, Part 1 of that journal in January, 1992, pp 5-31. Windsor has taken data from the boat-shaped formation in Turkey together with that set down in the Genesis account, to show, using a 'lofting' method, that the size and shape of the formation are consistent with the 300 × 50 × 30 cubit dimensions given in Scripture. Windsor also attempts to demonstrate the accuracy of his thesis by superimposing an overlay of the hull shape he has so formulated, upon the hull shape derived from on-site measurements drawn to scale. The correspondence between the two is remarkable.

23. D. Fasold, *The Ark of Noah*, p 255. The notion of the ark as a reed vessel covered with a bituminous mixture of cement was postulated long before Fasold suggested it. A.S. Yahuda in *The Accuracy of the Bible* (Heinemann: London, 1934), p 192, suggested that the ark was possibly composed of reed and a kind of bitumen.

24. Some who have been sceptical about this particular formation have suggested that it is not a man-made object but a natural geological formation, perhaps a syncline. In most instances the syncline idea has resulted from observing its appearance in photographs rather than from examining the formation itself. Appearances however can be very misleading as any careful researcher knows. Synclines *can* look like boats, but close scientific inspection that goes well beyond surface appearance generally reveals that they are not boats. Conversely, a boat *can* look like a syncline, especially if it happens to lie on a valley floor covered and surrounded by mud and is adjacent to, or impaled upon, what appears to be an igneous intrusion (as in the case of this formation). Careful examination of the site to date reveals that the formation lacks the major geological characteristics one would expect to find were it a syncline. For example, a syncline would consist of layers of strata which are dished or dipped towards its middle section. Where these layers are exposed in the outside walls they form quasi-horizontal bands around the formation. The Akyayla formation does not have such horizontal bands or bedding but has in fact vertical columns strongly suggesting that whatever it is, it is not a syncline. To postulate that these quite regularly spaced upright structures around the walls of the formation might *all* be vertically intrusive dykes would be fanciful to say the least. The suggestion that such structure is vertically bedded is also at odds with the subsurface indications of a *horizontal* planar reflector.

One academic was reported in the press as having travelled into the Australian outback and located a syncline there in an effort to prove the Akyayla formation is also a syncline. He and some others have suggested that the existence of boat-shaped natural formations, in other places such as on Mount Ararat, somehow indicates that the Akyayla formation is probably the same. Of course, such geological sameness can be established only by studying them *all*—not superficially but by investigating what is inside. Once we are certain what is *inside* the Akyayla formation, we can then compare it with what is *inside* the other formations, whether they be in Turkey or near Tibooburra in Australia.

Likewise, samples collected by anyone in the outback of Australia have little if any relevance to what is on a Turkish site until they are carefully analysed and compared with samples excavated from within the formation on that Turkish site. Until this has been done, we shall be dependent on data derived from non-invasive methods. To date much of the on-site data appears to be highly anomalous. The well-documented evidence of regular patterns of 'iron lines' along with other features presented in this book would certainly appear to be quite inconsistent with anything one would expect to find in a 'natural' geological formation. Unless these same features can be shown to occur within natural formations elsewhere, neither they nor the formation in which they exist can be confidently designated natural.

The next step in determining what the formation really is, is to dig it and find out what is inside. When this is done, it should be possible to determine whether what is there is natural or man-made.

25. D. Fasold, *The Ark of Noah*, p 89 ff; R. Wyatt, *Discovered: Noah's Ark!*, 1989, pp 9-10 and J. Baumgardner, *Noah's Ark?* official newsletter, Los Alamos, New Mexico, October 1985. Each of these three describes the team as comprising the two others and himself doing metal-detection work on the site. Further to this the author of this book has carefully examined video-tape footage of this, the first series of metal-detection surveys carried out on the site in 1985 and 1986. It features all three of these men working together. Sometimes they are seen working with their own detectors, each quite independent of the others but where necessary in vocal contact. The footage features also their procedures, comments and reactions to what they were detecting. This video tape is an official electronically screen-dated record of the work done in the form of a 'presentation being offered to the public by David Fasold' and is so designated in the introduction. Readers interested in gaining further information about the events and statements documented on this important video-tape should contact Mr David Fasold, The Noahide Society, 14781 Pomerado Rd., Poway CA 92064.

26. Dr Baumgardner is a geophysicist who held a post in the University of California Los Alamos National Laboratory.

27. These details were made available in the publications cited in note 25 and are also documented in a range of photographs and video tapes now held on file.

28. J. Baumgardner, op cit.

29. Ibid.

30. Anyone who examines this informative 'on location' video documentation (as cited above in note 25) will be able to ascertain for himself the
procedures used to locate and identify the patterns of iron. He will also be
able to hear Dr Baumgardner's assessment as a scientist of the evidence
which emerged from the survey, as well as his carefully framed conclusions,
based on that evidence, about designating the formation as man-made, a
boat and Noah's ark. Very specific information about the regular patterns of
these iron 'fittings' and laboratory results concerning them (using, for example, electron microscope scanning) was made available to the public via
United States television programmes such as 'Solved—Unsolved Mysteries'
hosted by Robert Stack. Data yielded on this occasion were also reported in
the US press. For example, the unusual pattern of lines revealed by this
metal-detector survey along with the techniques used to locate it were
reported in considerable detail in an article published in *The New American*, 17
December 1990. This article tells how, when the detector scanned the area
outside the perimeter of the formation, no iron was found; but when the area
inside it was scanned, some 5,400 separate spots, averaging one to every 8.16
sq ft of surface area, were located. When retested, each metal position was
flag-marked. Each was found to be on one of 14 longitudinal lines (from bow
to stern) or else on one of 9 transverse lines (from starboard to port).

31. J. Baumgardner, op cit.

32. Ibid.

33. J. Baumgardner (ibid) stated that prior to the arrival of a radar techni-
cian and David Fasold scheduled for 17 August 1985, an advance team would
survey the site, attempt some drilling and repeat the metal-detector scan.
Although the drilling process was not possible, Dr Baumgardner reported
that the metal-detector scan revealed once more the amazing pattern of lines
which he and his team marked using long plastic tapes and which he
recorded photographically for inclusion in the same newsletter. It has been
suggested in *Creation ex Nihilo*, vol 14 no 4, September/November 1992 in an
article by Dr Snelling that the 'iron lines' that were marked out with plastic
tapes were detected with a so-called 'molecular frequency generator/discrim-
inator' (ibid p 28 col 3 and p 29 col 4). However, Dr Baumgardner, in his
October newsletter where he describes these metal-detection surveys, makes
no mention of the use of this piece of equipment. The only term used by Dr
Baumgardner in this newsletter is 'metal detector', not 'molecular frequency
generator/discriminator'. David Fasold's video tape presentation (referred to
in note 25) shows him (David Fasold) actually confirming with witnesses the
earlier White metal-detector results. It *is* true that David Fasold used a
molecular frequency/discriminator (as well as an ordinary metal detector) to
locate on-site iron. However, it is also true, as video-tape evidence clearly
indicates, that the molecular frequency generator/discriminator appeared to

confirm the patterns located by the metal detectors. Leaving aside the question of the molecular frequency generator/discriminator's scientific validity and David Fasold's use of this equipment, one thing is clear; namely that on the latter occasion in August, when Dr Baumgardner found the metal patterns and marked them with bright yellow three-inch plastic tapes (as his October 1985 newsletter clearly states) David Fasold had not yet arrived to detect these patterns with his molecular frequency generator/discriminator (ibid, and also *The New American*, 17 December 1990, which makes mention of this and the fact that Dr Baumgardner had completed his own metal-detecting project on the site before David Fasold arrived). Ron Wyatt in *Discovered: Noah's Ark!* writes that the 'distinct linear subsurface pattern' detected in the earlier investigation was repeated in August of that year (p 17). The team comprised Dr J. Baumgardner, Ron Wyatt, Maylon Wilson, a scientist from Los Alamos Laboratories, and Tom Anderson, a lawyer from Indio, California. The fact that this visit was finished before David Fasold arrived is confirmed by Fasold himself (see *Ark of Noah*, p 121). It needs to be stressed in summary that ordinary metal detectors had picked up the pattern of lines *prior* to any use of the molecular frequency generator which confirmed that pattern.

34. It is abundantly clear from this written documentation and video footage that scientifically acceptable White metal-detectors of standard manufacture and commonly used were those employed for the early stages of the project to locate and establish with laboratory samples the presence of iron in linear patterns; and that these patterns were later reproduced and thereby confirmed in another metal-detector survey carried out and documented by Dr John Baumgardner, a highly experienced and responsible geophysicist.

35. 'JULY 1987 GEOPHYSICAL INVESTIGATION OF NOAH'S ARK (DURUPINAR SITE) MAHSER VILLAGE, DOGUBAYAZIT, AGRI, OFFICIAL REPORT SUBMITTED BY JOHN R. BAUMGARDNER, UNIVERSITY OF CALIFORNIA, LOS ALAMOS NATIONAL LABORATORY AND M. SALIH BAYRAKTUTAN, ATATURK UNIVERSITY FACULTY OF ENGINEERING, NOVEMBER 1987, ERZURUM, TURKEY.'

36. Ibid, p 2.

37. Ibid, Abstract. Further technical detail is also set out in the introduction. The geophysical instrumentation, including a SIR System-8 ground-penetrating radar manufactured by Geophysical Survey Systems of Hudson, New Hampshire. Fig 4 of the report shows the antenna unit used to transmit and receive the radar signals. The antenna was dragged across the site on transects spaced two metres apart. Radar pulses approximately 5 nano seconds in width were transmitted at a repetition rate of 50kHz. The return radar signal was recorded on magnetic tape and played back for visual inspection and interpretation on the graphic recorder. The survey was per-

formed during the period of 19-23 July 1987. Other instrumentation included a proton-precession magnetometer Model G-856A and a single-channel signal enhancement seismograph Model ES-125, both manufactured by EGG Geometrics of Sunnyvale, California. The magnetometer survey of the site was conducted 27-28 July by taking readings at two-metre intervals in both co-ordinate directions. Seismograph investigation of the site was performed 29-30 July. The results of these investigations are discussed in this report which is dated 10 November 1987, Erzurum.

38. Ibid, title page.

39. Ibid, Abstract and John Baumgardner *Is it Really the Ark?* official newsletter: Los Alamos NM, 15 September 1987.

40. Ibid.

41. J. Baumgardner and M. Salih Bayraktutan, *Geophysical Investigation of Noah's Ark*, Erzurum, Turkey, November 1987, p 10.

42. Ibid, pp 35, 45.

43. Ibid, p 45. Material at seismic velocity (2,400-3,300 m/s) lies at 6-8 m and the report suggests this is the same material responsible for the strong radar reflections at 4-8 m.

44. Ibid, CONCLUSIONS, p 49.

45. Ibid.

46. Ibid.

47. Ibid.

48. Ibid.

49. Ibid, ABSTRACT.

50. Ibid.

51. J. Baumgardner, *Is it really the ark?* official newsletter, 15 September 1987.

52. J. Baumgardner and M. Salih Bayraktutan, *Geophysical Investigation of Noah's ark*, ABSTRACT, p 10.

53. J. Baumgardner, op cit.

54. Ibid.

55. Ibid.

56. J. Baumgardner, *A Search For the Elusive Ark*, official newsletter, 19 August 1988.

57. Letter from Dr J. Baumgardner written in reply to an official letter 14 August 1992 from Mr John Farr, on behalf of the Sydney project organisers, regarding details of evidence from the Akyayla site elicited and interpreted by Dr Baumgardner. In this letter Dr Baumgardner gave details concerning the findings which emerged from the core drillings, namely:

● that there were four drillings taken: of these, the two taken along the centre line in the southern sector did not locate the planar reflector. Dr Baumgardner gave as the reason for this that those who did the work were unfortunately 'not able to drill enough holes in the area where the planar reflector occurred to make a definitive interpretation'. The question this raises is, where is the planar reflector layer? It would seem, as Dr Baumgardner himself states, it was simply not encountered.

● that the third core, also on the centre line (north of the outcrop), indicated that 'coherent basement rock extends all the way to the surface'. Again the planar surface was not encountered.

● that the fourth core hole on the eastern edge of the site revealed 'only mud-flow material for the full 10 metre depth'. Once more, the planar surface was not encountered.

Furthermore, additional information gained by Dr Baumgardner that a long ridge of coherent basement rock 'extends to within 10-15 feet of the surface along the centre line', dropping away from it 'in a transverse direction', indicates that this ridge does not have the profile required to enable it to be identified as the planar reflector revealed earlier by subsurface equipment.

58. 'There was no evidence from the core drillings for wood, petrified or otherwise.' J. Baumgardner, op cit.

59. Ibid.

60. Ibid. This ridge-shaped island of basement rock was the one which the drills had revealed along section of the centre line. Dr Baumgardner in his 15 September reply to Mr Farr's request for scientific evidences to support the notion that the formation might not be a man-made one, made reference to this island of basement rock located by three core-drillings. He referred to it in that letter as 'a strip of ophiolitic rock representing former ocean floor incorporated into the continental rocks along a zone of continental collision [which] happens to cut across the area and underlies the site'. Indeed, the object *is* in an ophiolitic zone (see p 100, *Introduction to Geology*, Vol 2, Read and Watson). However, this information does not preclude the formation's being a man-made object and is in fact quite consistent with that possibility if one assumes that the formation, if it were indeed once a boat, is not now in its original location having been transported from higher up the mountain (a

possibility Dr Baumgardner has himself mentioned—see earlier in note 41 ff). It must be stated that whilst continuing to stand by the data derived from his earlier research on the site, Dr Baumgardner has since modified his interpretation of that data and no longer holds to the position that the formation is a man-made object.

61. J. Baumgardner, *Is it Really the Ark?*, official newsletter, 15 September 1987.

62. Ibid.

63. Ibid. Dr Baumgardner's evidence seems to be contradicted by Dr Andrew Snelling who stated (see *Creation ex Nihilo* magazine, Vol 14 no 4 September/November 1992 article, p 2 cols 2 & 3) that 'The notable discovery of iron oxide (limonite) nodules in the surface mud is entirely consistent with the weathering of iron sulphide (pyrite) nodules and veins (which are found in the rocks of the area).' Dr Baumgardner, however, from his extensive work on the site explicitly states that these limonite nodules were not only anomalous but never observed anywhere in the fissures and mudflow clay (publication cited in note 61). These limonite nodules would therefore, in the light of so much metal having been detected on site, appear to be significant.

64. Ibid.

65. Ibid.

66. Prior to the author's first visit to the site, he had occasion when in Britain to study the archaeological findings which emerged at Sutton Hoo where an early medieval Anglo-Saxon ship had been buried under a mound. Details of the ship's structure were preserved in the corrosion products of its rivets. As each rivet corroded, 'the oxides migrated into the wood immediately surrounding the rivet and preserved it' (see A.C. Evans, *The Sutton Hoo Ship Burial*, British Museum Publications Ltd: London, 1989, p 25). The possibility that the limonite nodules found at the Akyayla site by core drilling have been formed in a similar manner should be seriously considered.

67. Late in the summer of 1990, Ron Wyatt, Richard Rives and others carefully inspected these structures. Their existence under the mud veneer was fully documented both photographically and on video tape. When the author was there in the following summer they were still observable and were photographed on that occasion also by a number of the team examining the site.

68. They appear to be highly unusual. Until examples of very similar or identical structures can be shown to exist in 'natural formations', there would seem to be a reasonable basis for assuming that they might be perhaps the metamorphosed ribs of an ancient boat, especially since they are spaced so regularly along the outside of this boat-shaped object.

69. This document headed 27 June 1991, states that the object was indeed

found on that occasion. It also states that Ron Wyatt was observed finding it and picking it up just outside the 'hull'. It is signed by Mr Foster Daniel, Mrs D. Barnes, Mr R. Murrell, and eight others including the author.

70. Galbraith Laboratories Inc, Knoxville TN, 18 July 1991, Assayers Laboratories, Elko NV, 16 September 1991 and Teledyne Allvac, Monroe NC where the taking of the sample and its testing were recorded on video tape by Mrs Mary Nell Wyatt of Nashville, Tennessee, who holds it currently on file. Scientists who were engaged in the testing also made their own photographic records with their own cameras and gave copies to Mrs Wyatt. Those involved in the analysis were very impressed by the fact that there were many times the amount of organic carbon present in the adjoining section sample as was found in the 'rivet' sample of the object. The test carried out at Teledyne Allvac, involved quantitative elemental analysis. More tests including thin sections on this sample and hopefully on others retrieved from the site are envisaged. Results will be published when all the necessary data are collated and evaluated.

71. The finding of this sample was witnessed by Dr Bulant Atalay, Mark Steffins, along with his wife and daughter, Hasan Ozer and 'Watcha' McCallum (now deceased).

72. Further tests including thin sections are planned before results are prepared for publication.

73. This sample has been visually identified as petrified wood by a number of geologists. It has been laboratory tested and awaits further scientific analysis, including thin sectioning, to determine its exact nature and whether its layers represent a form of *gophering* or lamination involving some kind of adhesive. This sample is being held on behalf of the Turkish Government and the results of further analysis will be made available for publication at the appropriate time.

74. Dr Smars, a medical doctor and veteran Ararat climber, together with Mr Bouma, an engineer and architect engaged by the Dutch Government in the historical restoration of windmills, made a valuable contribution to Mount Ararat research in 1990 by providing first-hand information to Dr D. Shockey and his team regarding an ice-cave formation that was under scrutiny that year as part of their helicopter investigation.

75. Jack Bouma was examining the area around the deck support when he noted the presence of this substance and reported it immediately to Dr Smars and the author who were examining fragments of igneous rock in the mud flow some fifty yards east of the formation. The substance was then photographed both *in situ* and in sample form. Small amounts of it were later laboratory analysed.

76. Positive identification of the sample as pitch was made on the basis of

analysis of a concentrated extract of the sample as submitted to Oil Check P/L, Sydney, New South Wales, Australia, and compared by them with a bitupave sample of bitumen (Tue 05 09:43:11 1991). The technique used was Fourier Transform Infra Red (FTIR). Contrary to Dr Snelling's comment on the analysis of this material (see *Creation ex Nihilo* article, Vol 14 no 4, September/November 1992, p 32, col 1), 'Gas chromatographic analysis' is *not* 'the only scientific procedure that could verify it as pitch.' Nor is it 'the standard method used' as Dr Snelling suggests. According to P. Duguid, M Sc (Pharm) of Robertson Scientific, the preferred method has always been IR (the infra-red technique) because 'the heavy long-chain carbon molecules' clog up the Gas Chromatographic column. Analytical trace and laboratory report are held on file by the author. Hopefully a dig will enable further samples of this substance to be located and examined.

77. According to testing at Galbraith Laboratories, Knoxville TN, 3 December 1984, a number of these samples contained over 80% Manganese Dioxide which, if they are indeed slag, could be the by-product of some metallurgical process. The designation of one of these samples by Dr A. Snelling (see *Creation ex Nihilo* article, Vol 14 no 4, September/November 1992, p 33, col 1) as possibly being an example of 'manganese nodules which even today are found on the ocean floor' would seem not to be sound, since such ocean floor nodules *never* attain this high percentage 80+% of manganese dioxide (see *Encyclopaedia Britannica*, 1985, 'Oceans and Seas' where it is stated that the content of manganese in such nodules is only 'as high as 50%'). Furthermore, the on-site chunks from which our samples were randomly taken were over a foot long—far too large to be manganese nodules, which (see *Oceans and Seas* as above) 'average only 4 cm'—slightly less than 2 inches. Therefore, because of its manganese dioxide content and its size, this material cannot be identified as ocean floor manganese nodules. It must be something else. One possibility (as Ron Wyatt suggests) is that the material might well be slag used perhaps as ship's ballast. This suggestion can be checked if more of the substance is found inside the formation on excavation. The notion of a high level of metallurgical sophistication prior to the Flood is suggested by the reference to Tubal-Cain in Gen 4:22.

78. A fossilised antler base was found within the perimeters of the formation whilst it was being inspected by a team accompanying Ron Wyatt prior to 1990. In 1991 the author also found another fragment—a small antler tip projecting out of the mud covering the mid-western section of the wall. The locating of this antler tip was witnessed by Mr Frank Barnes, an engineer, and his wife Mrs Debbie Barnes, a scientist, both of them in the group inspecting the site with many others. The object was detected in situ and photographed. The research required to deal with this object is underway but not yet completed. Unfortunately the object's significance cannot be properly determined until a number of things are done. Secure identification of the object must be established. Essentially this has been done. Additionally the species must, if at all possible, be identified biologically—no easy task, since

the object is only a small fragment. Once this is done the habitat of such an animal should be ascertained; not only its present but its past habitat. Having done this, it might then be possible to determine whether an animal of this species was ever indigenous to the region where the formation lies or whether it is exotic. Research into this area has already revealed that the area where the formation lies once abounded in various animals of many types. *The Life Nature Library Series*, ed. François Bourlière and the Editors of Life (Time-Life International, 1965), states,

> It is certain that palaeolithic man hunted deer, gazelle and goat 25,000 years ago in what is today Iran. Later...the pressure of larger grazing animals grew to the point where many faced extermination. The royal hunts in particular, carried on for over 2000 years were affairs of enormous slaughter. An Assyrian king of the 9th century BC boasted thus of his prowess... 'by my stretched-out arm, through my furious courage, 15 mighty lions from the mountains and the woods in my hand I captured...herds of wild oxen and elephants and lions and birds...beasts and wild asses and gazelles and stags...30 elephants...I slew and 250 mighty wild oxen I laid low and 370 mighty lions'. This same king gave a feast at which 500 deer and 500 gazelle were served in addition to 1,000 cattle and 1,500 sheep. The king also claimed that this same area provided the first sheep and goats to be tamed (p 27).

It is also indicated that the genetic parents of our modern wheat may well have come from this same general area.

If this ancient account is to be believed, it would seem that the spot where the formation rests was once in an area characterised by well developed pastoral and agricultural activities. In the light of this information, any evidence of the presence of animals, such as fragments of antlers, hooves or horns, must be assessed with caution. Such evidence, especially if it is found inside the boat-shaped formation, could be of real significance in establishing a positive identification of that formation. However, to establish such significance, a great deal more on-site investigation and interpretation of data will be necessary. Further on-site research is also required to discover whether there are other fragments—antlers, horns or hooves associated with the formation. Although this process is under way, there is still much more to be done before the significance of the object can be properly evaluated and the results published. At the time of writing, this research programme has been hampered by a serious lack of finances and dangerous terrorist activity in Eastern Turkey where the formation lies.

79. These await further scientific identification and analysis to determine animal type, food eaten and likely environment.

80. Provisional arrangements have now been made to have these and other samples of such hair forensically analysed to establish whether they are or were indigenous to this particular area. Hair can last for thousands of years without deterioration and still be capable of identification and analysis.

Determining the age of such samples is also important. However, this is by no means a straightforward matter. Unfortunately dating techniques are not as reliable as one would hope. Serious doubts have been raised by competent academics and researchers concerning for example radio carbon dating. (See Wakefield Dort, Dept of Geology, the University of Kansas, 'Mummified Seals of Southern Victoria Land', *Antarctic Journal* [Washington], Vol 6, September/October 1971, p 211 and Dr Allan Riggs, formerly of US Geological Survey, now on staff at University of Washington, Seattle, 'Major Carbon 14 Deficiency in Modern Snail Shells from Southern Nevada Springs', *Science*, Vol 224, 6 April 1984, p 58.) Documented research concerning the unreliability of the Rubidium Strontium method is provided by Dr C. Brooks, Professor of Geology, University of Montreal, Quebec, Canada, Dr D.E. James, Staff Member in Geophysics and Geochemistry, Carnegie Institute of Washington, Washington DC, USA, and Dr S.R. Hart, Professor of Science MIT—Massachusetts Institute of Technology, Cambridge, USA, 'Ancient lithosphere: Its role in young continental volcanism', *Science*, Vol 193, 17 September 1976, p 1093. The reliability of these and other methods of dating which might be relevant to this project are currently being evaluated.

81. An excellent illustration of an ancient Mesopotamian creel with three drogue stones (complete with rope holes), stacked on its deck is reproduced by André Parrot, Curator-in-Chief of The French National Museums, Professor Ecole du Louvre, Paris and Director of the Mari Archaeological Expedition, in his *The Flood and Noah's Ark*, translated from the French *Déluge et Arche de Noé* (Delachaux et Niestlé: Neuchâtel, 1953: and Camelot Press: London and Southampton, 1955). Honor Frost, world authority on anchor stones, presents a range of carefully researched material and photographs of these artefacts in *Arts et Industries de la Pierre*, Ras Shamra—Ougarit VI Sous la direction de Marguerite Yon, Editions Recherche sur les Civilisations, 1991 'Anchors Sacred and Profane', pp 356-408. Dr William Shea (once Professor of Old Testament at Andrews University, Berrien Springs, Michigan, now Associate Director of The Biblical Research Institute, Silver Springs, Maryland) examined the Arzap stones personally in Turkey and identified them as anchor stones (see his article in *CRS Quarterly*, pp 90-95, *Origins 82*, 1981).

82. *Urartu*, Accadian cognate of Ararat, used in ancient documents to designate Armenia which incorporated this range of mountains. *The Wycliffe Bible Commentary*, Old Testament, ed Charles F. Pfeiffer, Oliphants Ltd: London, 1963, p 14.

83. Gen 8:4. The Hebrew indicates that *mountains* is plural and that the ark rested *on* them.

84. *The Works of Flavius Josephus*, William Whiston MA (Ward Lock and Company: London, nd), I.iii.6. Thus Josephus suggests Armenia as the region where the ark landed. He also notes that the Armenians called the place where Noah, his family and the animals came out of the ark, *The Place of*

Descent. He adds that the remains of the ark 'being saved in that place...are shown there by the inhabitants to this day' (I.iii.5).

85. Charles Daly in his explanatory notes to the *Koran*, London, 1832, ch XI, pp 166-7, states that the name *Cardu* or *Gardu* given to the region was rendered by the Greeks as *Gordyaei*. Hence, the inhabitants were known as Gordyaeans or Cordyaeans.

86. Ibid, ch XI. The Mount Al Judi was constantly written by the Arabs for *Jordi* or *Giordi*. See also *The Travels of Marco Polo* (Heron Books, Edito-Service S.A. Geneva, published by arrangement with J.M. Dent, undated) footnotes pp 35 and 36, where confirmation of the Mohammedans' Al Judi, rather than Mt Ararat, occurs. 'L'opinion commune des Orientaux,' says D'Herbelot 'est que l'arche de Noé s'arrêta sur la montagne de *Gioudi*, qui est une des croupes du mont Taurus ou *Gordiaeus* en *Arménie*.' (See also this work ch 5, especially footnote 20.)

87. In 1990, the author, when asking the manager of Hotel Cimer where the ark landed, received the answer 'Al Judi' as he pointed towards the mountain ridge that overlooks the valley where the boat-shaped formation rests. (See also D. Fasold, *The Ark of Noah*, p 192, for further confirmation of local knowledge concerning this matter. Fasold gives other research evidence in this chapter to support the notion that this is in fact the mountain, Al Judi, cited by Mahomet in the *Koran*, as the landing-place of the ark.)

88. Gen 8:7 tells how the raven sent forth by Noah kept going to and fro until the waters had dried up from the earth. The name *Kargaconmaz* means 'Crow will not stand' (or 'perch'). Gen 7:7 states that there were eight humans on board the ark and for this reason the name *Village of the Eight* which is close by in this district is interesting.

89. Ron Wyatt and the author began to do this in their respective countries. In Australia the author maintained close contact with The Turkish Embassy in Canberra ACT and the Consulate in Sydney, NSW. The research, the projected plans to dig, protect and develop the site have been continuously shared with the appropriate government officials over a number of years. Applications have always been officially made through these authorities with embassy endorsement, then followed up with government personnel in Turkey and where necessary in Britain. All government representatives have been without exception extremely supportive.

90. Fax headed 1991-08-30/16:27, transmitted from Otel Oral, Erzurum, Turkey, to the author's son Chris Roberts and through him to the author's wife and various others listed.

CHAPTER

3

The Black Hell

The mountain spur which they were forcing us to climb was now very steep. My guard gripped my upper arm tightly as my feet dislodged rocks and sent them bounding down into the blue-black depths of the valley.

Strenuous climbing on the side of a mountain does peculiar things to the leg muscles; by now I was longing to walk on some level ground. So I was glad when my guard led me up on to a narrow rock and mud ridge which ran around the contour of the slope. I realised as soon as I began to walk on it that it was a kind of retaining wall built by local farmers to channel a natural watercourse around the side of the mountain. This little raised footpath made the ascent much easier, but only for a short time. It soon became too dangerous to walk on when its downhill side sloped steeply away to become a rocky precipice. I knew that there'd be no second chance for anyone who slipped off that ridge.

Our only alternative now was to slosh along knee-deep in this muddy little creek. My guide led me down into its gurgling waters and we began to move upstream.

Although my feet were soon soaking wet, I was glad that my boots afforded protection from the sharp rocks and roots of the creek bed.

Just ahead of us poor Gary, with nothing on his feet but sandals, was making very heavy weather of it. I could see him gingerly trying to feel his way over a surface he could not see as his guard kept urging him forward.

After ten minutes or so, he stopped. Even in the dark I could tell from his hunched, motionless stance there in the stream that he had injured himself. His guard helped him as he hop-climbed out of the water and up on to the steep bank. He had lacerated his foot.

Apparently his guard did not consider it serious enough to warrant either delay or treatment, so in a few moments we were all wading on again. When we finally stopped for a brief rest, it was possible to see the summit of the range, just a few hundred feet higher.

We were about to leave the stream and climb up to it when Ron and his guard caught up with us. I was disturbed by Ron's condition. He was breathing heavily and stumbling as he made his way up the slope between the trees. His guard was trying to help him, but Ron seemed oblivious to him or anyone else. The exertion of the climb had brought the big man to the threshold of physical exhaustion.

It was obvious once again that our captors were not going to be slowed down by such matters; so on we went. Gary, supported by his guard, hobbled as fast as he could up the steep incline towards the summit and Ron, near collapse, stumbled from tree to tree.

Before we attained the summit, I witnessed a procedure which was to be repeated numerous times on subsequent marches. Everyone was given the silent 'shhh' signal, and as we all stood stock still the guerrilla leader imitated the night chirp of an insect, or sometimes the call of a bird. The same call was returned by the guerrilla who had been sent ahead on reconnaissance. The coast was clear, it seemed, so we were silently motioned forward.

In another ten minutes or so, we had topped the thickly forested summit and were being led downhill into a little clearing where several other guerrillas were awaiting us.

There was a great deal of animated conversation among our captors as we arrived. This was quickly followed by a most unpleasant time of interrogation—our second for the evening. Some of the young men who had not yet met us gathered around. Then one of them fixed his gaze on Richard. He narrowed his eyes, and pointing at him said,

'*Emerikan!* CIA!'

'No! No!' Richard responded, holding his open hands each

side of his head and shaking hands and head together, 'No CIA! No CIA!' he protested.

Another of them pointed accusingly at him and said, '*Emerikan militery! militery!*'

'No military! No military—archaeology!' Richard countered.

They then turned their attention to Marvin, flinging similar accusations at him—this time adding the name of George Bush.

Like Richard, Marvin also denied all such associations, lest he be deemed a spy.

When Gary limped into the clearing it was his turn. To the accusation that he was an American, he responded with all the quiet, old-fashioned dignity of the true Celt. He simply announced that he was British. When they asked him whether he had been in the army, he nodded and held his head high. At that moment it would not have been difficult to imagine Gary with nineteenth-century side-whiskers and moustache, wearing his red jacket and white army helmet, all ready to break into *Men of Harlech* as the Welsh tenors did at Yorke's Drift.

Wisely, Gary went on to explain that he had been in the army a long time ago. He sought to express this fairly crucial piece of information in his quite respectable Turkish. For some reason he got away with it. They didn't shout at him as they had shouted at me earlier that evening.

I was not questioned at all. Perhaps they were satisfied that I was indeed an Australian; perhaps, with my grey beard, I looked enough like a professor to pass muster.

Suddenly Ron came into view. His appearance disturbed us all. His arms hung limply over the shoulders of two guerrillas who were almost dragging the bulk of his large frame towards us.

He was barely conscious as we took him from them and carefully lowered him to the ground.

He lay there motionless. His breathing became very shallow— almost undetectable. Gary could not find his pulse. After a minute or two he stirred and weakly gasped out a request to lift up his head for a bit. As Ron lay there so still, the terrible thought that he might die assailed me. I thought of his wife Mary Nell and of her unutterable sense of loss if he did. As I looked at his motionless grey-bearded face and tousled hair, I became horri-fyingly aware, too, that the prodigious amount of archaeological knowledge stored in this remarkable man's head would be lost the instant he died—lost to each of us and to the world.

I suspected that similar thoughts were coursing through Richard's and Marvin's minds. They had both worked before with Ron in the Middle East and knew that he was arguably the most informed researcher on the Nuh'un Gemisi project in the world today. Gary, of course, was not yet aware that this man, whose pulse he so desperately sought, was one of the world's great adventurer-archaeological researchers. As far as our Kurdish captors were concerned, Ron was just one of five Westerners who had some political bargaining value; on-the-hoof livestock in some weird ideological meat-market.

While we were all huddled anxiously around Ron, the guerrillas squatted in small groups or stood around smoking and chatting. Suddenly Ron began to stir.

Marvin, who had just taken over from Gary, announced that he had found Ron's pulse.

'I can feel it,' he said, staring into the distance as he concentrated hard, 'but it's threaded...'

Then Ron spoke.

'Lift my head up for a bit,' he gasped weakly.

I slipped in behind him and as the others gently lifted the upper part of his body, supported his shoulders and head against my chest. In a few minutes he was beginning to breath more normally. However, I was concerned that our captors might make us push on again before Ron was ready. I feared that if they did, the stress might cause another collapse; this time perhaps with a heart attack—even a fatal one. I prayed that Ron would be protected and preserved from these things. We sat there for an hour or so. During this time Ron began to improve.

While we waited, I listened to the guerrillas. They all seemed to be speaking in Kurdish, but once or twice I fancied I heard a couple of them using French. I thought this strange, since French is rarely spoken by the locals in Eastern Turkey. In the west it is more common, especially in large cities such as Istanbul. When I was in Europe prior to my first trip to Turkey, I remember asking a Frenchman who had travelled in Turkey whether my French would be handy there; especially in the Eastern provinces. He assured me that if I had both English and French, I would have no problems with communication in that region. I was comforted by this information since my Turkish at that time was fairly rudimentary. It turned out to be misleading information. When I arrived in Eastern Turkey, I found that very few people spoke English and virtually no one spoke French. In fact the only person with whom I spoke French during my entire visit was a young man I met in Erzurum on my way home. He was a bell-hop in a hotel there who carried my bags up to my room. So much for the value of my five hard years of schoolboy French!

I wondered where these French-speaking Kurds had been recruited from. Perhaps there might be some value in knowing what they were saying and at some stage having a common vehicle of communication with them.

Eventually, our captors provided us with some Turkish tea served in its little glass cups. As they handed it to us they called it *çay*, but stressed the fact that it was *Kurdi çay*. They handed us small lumps of sugar which we dropped in and dissolved by stirring them around with dry oak twigs. While we were sipping our tea, one of the guerrillas took from his knapsack several folded pieces of thin unleavened bread which is a staple food throughout the Middle East. This bread is known in Turkey as *ekmek*. These folded quadrants of *ekmek* opened up into very large floppy circular pancakes; quite enough when torn apart and passed around to provide us all with a sustaining snack.

We had barely finished this little meal when we were ordered to form up again into our marching column. Each of us had two guards this time—one in front and one behind. One of Ron's guards supported him as he stood up and led him into the column just in front of me. The second guard stood behind Ron. Gary, still trying to keep the weight off his lacerated foot, was led into the column by one of his guards.

We headed off down the mountain. The slope was steep. The undergrowth was dense. We were being led down into the foothills of a very wide valley which extended out to our right. On the floor of this valley, away in the distance, the dim lights of two villages glowed. It was perfectly clear that we were not heading towards the villages. They were keeping us close to the mountains.

As we wound our way down through the trees, dogs from a nearby farm began to bark. Every now and then I caught a glimpse of Ron down the slope ahead of me. As far as I could make out, he seemed to be doing all right; of course, this stint was all downhill so far.

However, in the next few minutes that was all to change. We suddenly found ourselves walking along a gravel road which wound quite steeply up into the mountain range.

I could see after a while that Ron was beginning to have trouble walking again. The guard assisting him did not slow his pace and Ron, who has a reputation for stubborn persistence, pressed on without complaint. As the incline steepened, I could see, as I had seen earlier in the evening, that Ron was beginning to stumble.

To my surprise, the guard who was supporting him looked over his shoulder towards me and asked me in French whether he was sick.

'*Est-il malade?*'

'*Oui,*' I replied quickly, '*Il est malade, très malade—sérieux!*'

Then, tapping the left side of my chest to indicate my heart, I added, '*C'est le coeur, le coeur!*'

I was surprised that this young man should have any doubts that Ron was really sick, in the light of his earlier and present symptoms. Perhaps they thought he was feigning illness.

Whatever they thought, they were not about to stop, but maintained the same brisk pace. However after a quick exchange of remarks, both of Ron's guards began to support him. The road we were following wound up and around the foothills of a long valley. There were no downhill sections. The gradient was constant and steep.

Eventually they made a brief 'comfort stop'; Marvin, whose stomach had been upset when we started our minibus trip, was now suffering from a severe gastric upset.

He was still not well when he returned to the column with his guard, but in spite of this he decided to help Ron along. So when we moved off again, there was Ron, as before, pressing on valiantly in front of me, supported by a Kurd on one side and an American on the other. Middle East and West had come together in a sort of joint project—a bit like the recent Gulf War, I thought.

As we tramped on, I observed the difficulty Ron was experiencing and knew that all I could do was pray that he'd have strength enough for each step and the physical resilience not to collapse again, or worse, suffer that fatal heart attack.

For an hour, we tramped on and on, higher and higher into this seemingly endless valley.

After our next stop, I slipped in under Ron's left arm.

'How are you doing, Ron?' I asked.

'OK,' he breathed.

'Been praying you along,' I added.

'Thank ya kindly, pilgrim,' he panted as he squeezed my arm.

'You know, Ron,' I said, 'you were saying only yesterday that you needed to lose a lot of weight. I reckon this is a quick way for you to do it.'

'Sure is,' he drawled in that bass voice of his, 'so long as I don't lose the whole 228 lbs in one go.'

It was getting on to 2 am when we reached the head of the valley. Here the road curved to our left and ran down alongside a little farm in a hollow.

We were cautioned to pass by silently. Though we tried our best to do so, we still set the dogs barking. As we left the flat-roofed stone farmhouse behind us, I wondered whether its occupants were hostile or sympathetic to the PKK cause. If they were hostile, then what could they do when confronted by twenty heavily armed guerrillas? After a little reflection it seemed fairly obvious to me that they would be sympathetic.

Suddenly, we left the road and began to climb up towards the top of the adjacent mountain range. We headed towards a little conical outcrop of rocks; no cover under which to hide, but a good vantage point. On reaching this spot most of the guerrillas slipped off their knapsacks. Their guns stayed with them. A few of them stood guard as the rest of us made ourselves as comfortable as we could between or on the rocks. By this time and at this altitude the temperature had dropped considerably and a very cold breeze was blowing. I pulled up the collar of my army jacket and zipped up the front as high as it would come under my chin. Then, like everyone else, I tried to snatch some sleep. Before I dropped off, one of the guerrillas took a thin blanket from around his waist and threw it over me. He also pushed his knapsack under my head with the one word, 'Professor'. With my hand I made a small 'eyebrow' salute and fell asleep.

After barely half an hour we were on the way again. In Indian file, as before, we came down from the little outcrop and crossed over a shallow valley. Then we began to ascend a tree-covered prominence which appeared to be the highest point on this part of the mountain. From it, one would have a commanding view of the surrounding country in all directions.

After pausing to send and receive the appropriate reconnaissance signals, we all began to spiral up towards the summit. Just below the highest point was a small clearing among the oak saplings. We stopped there. It was to be our camp site for the rest of the night.

A number of guards were posted as sentries on the slopes below our camp. Two others took charge of us. The rest of the guerrillas moved to a higher section of the clearing where they lay down to sleep.

We five were tossed a few small threadbare blankets and haversacks for pillows then directed to lie down under the saplings.

As unpleasant as it was to retire for the night under the muzzle of a loaded gun, none of us stayed awake to worry about it. The exhaustion of the previous seven hours claimed us quickly. It seemed almost no time at all before dawn broke. The camp was already alive with activity. Our guards were changed over, as were several others who had been posted around the slopes below us.

From the pat-pat-pat sound higher up in the clearing, we knew that the daily *ekmek* ration was being prepared for baking. Under the trees nearby two young men were gathering and breaking sticks for a fire. They carefully examined each one to ensure that it would not produce smoke.

Another young man was digging a neat square hole in the clay; the first stage in making a 'guerrilla fire'. When sticks were brought to him, he laid them down in a square formation around the hole, in much the same way as we used to do as children when we built log cabins or pigsties out of matchsticks. When the structure was about a foot high, he laid a few pieces of paper in the bottom and covered them with thin dry twigs. Then taking a cigarette lighter (they all had them, and smoked heavily) he flicked it and held the flame under the corner of a white woven-fibre plastic sack. As the bottom edge of the sack began to burn with a blue flame, he held it over the paper in his little fireplace.

The burning plastic dripped off in little globules of blue flame, the paper ignited and the fire was soon blazing—without smoke.

Breakfast consisted of small slices of tomato and cucumber with *ekmek*. It was placed before us on a tin plate which sat on a folded white-fibre plastic bag. I noticed that we were served our meal before any of the guerrillas received theirs.

Before we began to eat, we bowed our heads and quietly thanked God for the food. We also thanked him briefly for preserving our lives so far, and asked that he would take care of our families and perhaps in some special way touch the hearts of our captors. When we had finished this plain but wholesome fare, we were served *çay*, again with small lumps of sugar.

Afterwards we were directed by our guard to hide ourselves under the saplings. As we lay there we could hear guerrillas monitoring news bulletins on their radio. They were obviously expecting to hear reports of their having kidnapped us.

After an hour or so, the sun became very hot. By mid morning it was difficult to find a cool spot anywhere in the dappled shade. Still weary from the previous night's exertion, we tried as best as we could to get some sleep. Those guerrillas who were not now posted as sentries crawled into their own little shady spots and began to doze off as well.

The sentries who stood guard, though, never took their eyes off us for a moment. They never talked. They never smoked and nothing escaped their notice. When it was necessary for us to visit the area designated for use as a latrine, we had to get permission to go there from one of them. He would then accompany us, positioning himself where he could scrutinise our every action.

What nefarious plans did these people think we could possibly indulge in on these occasions? The possibilities seemed pretty limited, I thought…Perhaps we might be burying stolen weapons in the holes we had dug and covered up. Or perhaps the numerous leaves we picked ostensibly as toilet tissue substitutes would be stashed in our pockets and later used as fuel for a signal fire. Such a close scrutiny was somewhat embarrassing, to say the least, for the first few times.

By eleven o'clock the heat was becoming really oppressive. Marvin, Richard, Ron and myself found a reasonably shady spot and sat there fairly close together. We were therefore able to chat quietly. We did this discreetly, being careful not to say anything

that might arouse suspicion. Although it did not seem at this
point that any of our captors could understand English, we were
by no means certain that this was so.

I looked across the clearing at Gary and wondered how he was
faring. He was lying on his back with his head propped up on a
mini-haversack he had been carrying when we were first captured. He had pulled up one leg of his *şalvar* and was sunning the
gash in his foot.

I asked one of our guards to let me go to the latrine area. On
my way back I sat down next to Gary to chat with him.

'How's the foot, Gary?' I asked.

'Oh, it's not too bad, you know,' he answered. 'I think it will
be all right. How is Ron, Allen?' he added with much concern.

'A lot better than he was last night,' I replied. 'He'll be OK if
they don't walk us like that again.'

'I wonder what they plan to do with us?' asked Gary.

'Who knows?' I replied. 'Depends on what their aim was in
taking us, I guess.'

'They kidnapped several Germans a little while back. Did you
know that?'

'Yes, I did hear something about it,' I said.

'They released them after ten days.'

'Perhaps they'll do the same with us after they've made some
political capital out of us,' I commented.

'Oh, I do hope it won't be long,' he said.

'Me, too,' I added. 'If they hold us captive for more than a
week or ten days, we won't be able to do our preliminary dig.'

'What are you planning to dig?'

'A big, boat-shaped formation in the mountains near
Dogubayazit—looks as though it could be the remains of Noah's
ark. Unless these fellows release us pretty soon, we'll not be able
to do our dig before winter comes.'

'Do you really think it's Noah's ark?' asked Gary.

I had been asked this question many times before in the course
of my research on the project and decided early on that the
question of what I *thought* was really immaterial to the real issue.
The ultimate question seemed to me to be one of evidence,
namely: Do we have archaeological evidence that this large, boat-
shaped formation is consistent with the description of Noah's ark

as described in the Old Testament accounts? On that basis, I answered Gary's question:

'Well, this thing is in the right place: 6,300 feet above sea level on the mountains of Ararat. And it seems to be about the right length according to the measurements taken. So if it's not the ark we'd like to know what it is. That's the reason the four of us came to Turkey—to excavate it and find out for sure.'

We both lay there in the silent midday heat.

'Gary, you said you came to Turkey for a holiday. Is this your first visit?'

'Oh, no,' he said, 'I've been here several times before.'

'You must like the place.'

'Yes, I do—particularly the area around Lake Van. I was so looking forward to going there again.'

After a few moments reflection, he added distantly, 'I'm not sure I'll be strong enough to withstand the stress of all this.'

'I don't see why,' I said. 'You're coping as well as any of us. Why do you say that, Gary?'

'I've just recently come out of a nervous breakdown,' he said.

He told me how a while back he'd been devastated by the loss of a job in which he had been secure and highly efficient over many years. Then, in the midst of this trauma, he had had to cope with the death of his aged mother for whom he had cared throughout a long-term illness. He went on to describe how, as a result of all this, he had withdrawn into a state of deep depression for about a year. Having just begun to emerge from this, he had decided to come to Turkey for a holiday.

'You know, Gary,' I said in a joking attempt to cheer him up, 'some people spend their holidays on expensive health farms—where they exhaust themselves on gruelling physical exercise programmes and torture themselves with diets of the plainest food imaginable. Let's look on the bright side, Gary. We're getting the same thing right here in this glorious mountain setting—and not paying a penny for it!'

My point about food was no sooner made than illustrated. Our free lunch was about to be served. Gary and I went over to the others where we sat down to a meal just like the one we'd had for breakfast.

After we'd finished eating, one of the young guerrillas handed us a small tape-player on which he'd been playing Kurdish music; jangly, highly rhythmical songs calculated to stir Kurdish sentiments. We had played a few of the songs by the time he'd returned. He squatted down near us with his elbows on his knees. Marvin handed the tape player back to him.

'*Tammum?*' asked the young man as he took it.

'*Tammum,*' we answered.

He seemed pleased and as he tapped his recorder, said, '*Kurdi! Tammum!*'

About mid-afternoon we heard an aircraft approaching. It seemed to be travelling in a straight line. Not long afterwards we heard other aircraft noises—some close and others further off. Some of them sounded like helicopters. These noises continued on and off throughout the entire afternoon. It seemed that the search for us had begun.

Every hour, on the hour, the guerrillas continued to use their radio to scan a range of news bulletins as they'd done earlier. Then later in the afternoon, to our surprise, they left their radio with us. We tried to pick up English-speaking stations which might report our plight. After an hour or more of unsuccessful dial-twiddling, we suddenly located a news bulletin which was being broadcast in French. Through the static, we heard the words '*cinq touristes,*' 'hostages' and 'minibus'. It sounded like us all right, even though they had wrongly assumed that we were all tourists. It would be only a matter of time now before information about us would be broadcast worldwide.

Just before dusk the group began to make preparations to move out. Everything was quickly and efficiently packed. Rubbish was buried under the trees. The latrine area was flattened then strewn with leaves. The square camp-fire hole was filled in and tamped down with a shovel. Then every guerrilla began to check his gun. I watched as magazine clips were removed, checked, filled with bullets then snapped back into place with the heel of the hand. The sounds of all this, together with the clicks of safety catches and cocking mechanisms, echoed throughout the campsite. These sounds, which had been programmed into me from boyhood as potentially dangerous, had a subconsciously disquieting effect upon me.

We were then placed in line, as before, and marched out. As we were leaving I noticed two guerrillas dragging leafy branches over the entire camp area to remove every trace of our having been there. As we moved down the slope in single file, we could hear the 'swish-swish' of those branches, now being used to sweep away our tracks.

After about ten minutes we descended into a dry creek-bed. The young man leading our column was the same man who had shouted so menacingly at us when we were first captured. When he gave the signal to stop, we all stood in line between our guards. The leader glanced at his wrist-watch. Then he took out a cigarette, lit it and began to smoke. After a couple of minutes he glanced at his watch again. Someone handed him the radio. He pulled up its aerial, turned up the volume and began a station-search. As he looked down at the dial, he narrowed his eyes to keep out the smoke that languidly and erratically dawdled up from his cigarette. He, too, was seeking a news report of the kidnapping and had broken our journey to stop and listen to it.

Guerrilla listening to BBC broadcast of kidnapping

It reminded me of the way, years ago, folk who lived in the outback of New South Wales would bring everything to a grinding halt to listen to their radios. Their interest was not in news bulletins, but in *Blue Hills*, a serialised saga of country folk just like themselves. As a young man, I can still remember being part of a car convoy filled with sweltering outback folk who stopped in the middle of a saltbush and red sand desert so they could give their undivided attention to the current episode of Gwen Meredith's *Blue Hills*.

The level of concentration displayed by our guerrilla leader as he listened to this broadcast would have done credit to the most avid Gwen Meredith fan. Indeed, every guerrilla in the column listened to this Turkish news report with the same rapt attention.

Their faces began to light up as the same words we had picked up earlier in French began to emerge now in Turkish. We also heard additional words such as 'PKK' and 'terrorist'.

By the time the newsflash was over, the leader was jubilant. He repeated the words 'PKK' and 'terrorist' and smote his breast. Then, holding the radio aloft, he pointed to it and proclaimed with immense satisfaction and pride,

'BBC! BBC!'

He then delivered an enthusiastic little speech to the group in Kurdish. Its purpose was undoubtedly to stress the political significance of this major media achievement. The name Kurdistan was mentioned several times.

Clearly, this BBC report of our kidnapping was seen as a means of focusing world attention on the PKK's demands for an independent sovereign Kurdistan.

If this kind of media coverage had been their aim in taking us hostage, then they had achieved it in less than twenty-four hours.

'On this basis,' I thought, 'there would be no reason for them to hold us any longer.'

Surely our release would now be imminent—maybe tonight?

CHAPTER

4

Human Shields

Having listened to the BBC news, our column moved on down through the little creek-bed. Within half an hour we had entered a broad valley. Along its undulating floor ran a well-maintained gravel road. We were not allowed to march on this road, however, but for some reason were made to walk beside it. Behind us, two guerrillas brushed away our footprints as they had done earlier in the evening.

I was still holding on to the possibility that our captors might release us now that we had served our political purpose. Perhaps that was why they had brought us to this road. Their plan, I thought, was probably to leave us at some point a little further on with instructions to walk to the next village, thus giving them plenty of time to withdraw unpursued into the mountains again. On the other hand, their aim might be to take us to some nearby village where we would be required to stay for a day or so until they made their getaway. As I looked down the road and out to either side there was no sign of a village, or even a single farmhouse. The only building in sight was way off to our right, high on a craggy hilltop. It had steep walls, and, although it was too dark to be sure, looked to me like one of Turkey's many ancient fortresses.

After trudging silently on for some two hours, we suddenly left the road and headed up diagonally on to a broad sloping tract of land which was eroded by a network of dry creek-beds.

If their aim was to release us, then why were they taking us off in this direction—back towards the mountains?

I was beginning to feel the frustration of being totally under the control of a group of people who were under no obligation to tell us anything about their plans for us. What I had been foolishly doing, of course, was grasping at bits of quite inadequate information and using them to come to the wrong conclusions.

I was disconsolately turning these thoughts over in my mind when I heard the distant sound of an approaching motor vehicle—probably a truck of some sort.

The noise galvanised our group leader into instant action. With his left arm he made a large 'follow-me-quickly' gesture, raising his forefinger to his lips, then turned and headed off over the rough stony ground. The rest of us followed as rapidly and quietly as we could.

From the roar of its motor, we could tell that the vehicle was quite close now. As it topped the crest of a small rise, its headlights illuminated the road behind us. Then, with a downward whine through a succession of gears, it came to a stop with a thin squeal of brakes. It was no more than 150 yards from us now. Over the 'chug-chug-chug' of its diesel engine, we could hear several male voices.

Was this a Turkish Army truck or a police vehicle sent out to search for us? If it were either, then in a matter of moments, we could all be caught up in a deadly shoot-out.

Paradoxically, I found myself hoping that if these were Turkish soldiers sent out to rescue us that they would not find us.

As we all scrambled up and down the banks of numerous creek-beds, we heard the 'clunk' of the truck's reverse gear being engaged.

I glanced quickly over my shoulder and saw that the headlights of the truck were beginning to sweep across towards us.

The group leader, who was only a few yards in front of me at the head of the column, waved me up on to the high ground where he was standing. As I approached, he turned and headed down into the next gully. The moment I began to follow him, a beam of light from the truck swept across us. Momentarily everything dazzled with incandescent brightness.

I was sure we had all been seen. I knew as I headed down into the darkness of the next gully that there was now a real possibility of our being pursued and mistakenly shot by Turkish soldiers.

For me as an Australian, this possibility had a bizarre twist to it. Over seventy-five years ago my mother, along with many others, was attacked by terrorists from Turkey. This happened not in Turkey but in her homeland, Australia. This remarkable incident is now known as the Battle of Broken Hill.

It seems that during World War I two Turks (though there is some doubt about their precise nationality), decided to declare war upon a party of picnickers travelling in open trucks into the country near Broken Hill. They opened fire on men, women and children, killing and wounding several with high-powered rifles. My mother escaped uninjured, but a young girl who lived in her neighbourhood was shot dead, as were several other passengers. After the attack the terrorists made off into the hills on the outskirts of the city where they were pursued and ultimately killed by Australian soldiers.

Were certain details of a 1915 news release about to be curiously reversed in a 1991 version?

'1 January 1915: Two Turkish men shot as terrorists by Australian soldiers; 31 August 1991: Australian man mistakenly shot as terrorist by Turkish soldiers.'

With all the strength our weary legs could summon we pressed on into the night, expecting at any moment to hear the ominous sound that would mark the beginning of a military confrontation. What would that sound be? An order to the guerrillas to surrender? A burst of machine-gun fire?

The sound which did emerge was totally unexpected. It was the sound of a woman's voice.

Women in Eastern Turkey, unlike those of certain other countries, are not involved in army or police operations of this kind. So this vehicle could not be an army or police truck, and would most likely belong to a farm owner or a private family. The sound of this one woman's voice defused the situation almost immediately. The terrible tension we had all been experiencing began to dissipate.

Another thirty minutes trekking brought us to a thickly wooded little valley. We climbed down into it and began to head up along its dry bed. We had not gone far when thick vegetation, trees and rocks made walking painfully slow. As we pushed on through the undergrowth a high-pitched squeal suddenly echoed against the walls of the little canyon. My first thought was that it was an anguished cry of pain from one of our number who had been badly injured. However, when the squeal was repeated a second or two later, I recognised it as the cry of an animal. One of the guerrillas had captured a wild goat which was now thrashing about in the bushes. I caught a glimpse of the terrified animal being restrained by the neck, as it tried frantically to scramble free over the rocks.

A mere ten minutes later, it became obvious that we would not be able to climb out of this steep-sided little valley, and so the leader decided that we should retrace our steps.

By about 10 pm we found ourselves close to the place where we had started. The valley was very narrow here, but difficult as it was to lie on a clay bank at an angle of some thirty degrees, we somehow managed it and were soon asleep.

Around midnight I was awakened by a burning sensation in the soles of my feet. A 'guerrilla fire' was blazing in the narrow creek-bed less than three feet from my boots, the soles of which were now too hot to touch. Except for those tending the fire and standing guard, everybody seemed to be asleep, so I found a spot on the bank between Richard and Gary and began to doze off again.

When I awoke, several guerrillas were sitting around the fire. Two more were preparing a meal of *ekmek* and tomato.

When we had all finished this simple meal and were sipping our *çay*, I noticed a man whom I could not recall having seen before. He was sitting cross-legged on the other side of the fire and was leaning forward to light his cigarette on its embers. He was several years older than the other guerrillas; probably in his mid-thirties. Something in his general demeanour suggested to me that he was, right now, the leader of the group.

His unshaven face was sharp-featured and gaunt. His high cheekbones were prominent and strong, whereas his thin receding lower lip and jaw gave the impression of weakness. The face was nonetheless a strong one, mainly because of the eyes. Though narrow—little more than slits—they glinted with a compelling dynamic intensity.

When he had finished his cigarette, he tossed it into the fire. Then, as every good host does in Turkey, he offered us some more *çay* and began (within our mutual language limitations) to engage us in conversation.

It was an ideological conversation from the very outset; a kind

**Ibrahim,
the 'General'**

of lecture to provide us with a number of insights into the current
political situation in Eastern Turkey. Predictably, he chose the
subject of George Bush as an appropriate place to start. He
pointed out with a range of ingenious gestures that the American
people, of which Ron, Marvin and Richard were fine and upright
examples, were *'tammum'*. George Bush, on the other hand, was
certainly not *'tammum'*.

So keen was he to make this point that he even descended to
the politically taboo English phrase 'no problem' to do it.

'*Emerikan* people—no problem, no problem!'

'George Bush—problem!'

He then sought to explain, by lining up his two index fingers
side by side, that George Bush was at one with the Turkish
military; the PKK's sworn enemy.

He went to great pains to ensure that we five thoroughly
understood who the real terrorists were.

'PKK—no terrorist, no terrorist!'

'*Militery*—terrorist! George Bush—terrorist!'

He tried to make a number of other points, most of which were
rather too complex for him to explain and for us to understand.
One of his grievances was that there was no Kurdish dictionary
currently available—a result, possibly, of the earlier ban on use
of the Kurdish language in Turkey.

As I watched and listened, I formed the impression that here
was a man of no mean ability. His attempt to communicate
difficult political concepts, when we had almost no language with

which to do it, said a great deal about him. I could also imagine him making his point militarily if he had to, even without the most basic weaponry.

I sensed as well that there was in him a commitment to his cause that would make him fight with an almost demonic fury. This feeling was heightened as the flickering light of the fire illuminated his face from below; ghoulishly accentuating its shadows and the upward sweep of his dark eyebrows.

Sitting close by me was a young guerrilla in his late twenties. In softly-spoken Kurdish he gave some brief instructions to two young men near the fire. They immediately stood up and climbed to the top of the creek bank. Here they began to break off leafy branches from the saplings growing there.

Were these branches to be used as brooms to erase our tracks again? As more and more of them were removed, each with a resounding crack, it was clear that they were to be used for some other purpose. After a little while, they dragged about ten of the branches down into the creek bed. At a spot about six feet from the fire they arranged them into a thick leafy mattress.

While this was being done, the guerrilla sitting next to me drew a long hunting knife from the leather scabbard attached to his belt. He laid its blade gently across the pads of his fingertips and tested it for sharpness with his thumb.

Cries from the goat captured earlier in the evening suddenly reverberated through the valley as the two guerrillas man-handled and dragged him by his tether towards us. In a matter of seconds their expert hands had tossed the creature, wriggling and squealing, on to the mattress of leaves where he was held immobile, ready for the knife.

The animal was slaughtered, bled and butchered with consummate skill.

The knife flashed in the firelight as it deftly laid bare and severed the edible parts of the carcase. As soon as each piece was removed, it was handed to the men whose job was to prepare and cook it. Delicacies such as kidneys, heart and liver, together with a variety of red meat cuts, were sliced up into tiny square pieces. A number of them were soon sizzling over the fire.

In the meantime, some young men had been busily whittling straight little sticks into shishkebab skewers and were now removing the bark from each and sharpening it at one end. When the meat was ready to be served, the cooks impaled each diced piece on its skewer. The sound, sight and smell of cooked meat stimulated our salivary glands into healthy activity. Although I suspected that this goat meat would taste wild and be rather chewy, it would nevertheless provide, I thought, a welcome variation from our diet of tomato, cucumber and *ekmek*.

They wrapped each skewer of meat, together with a few pieces of tomato, in a piece of *ekmek*. As each piece was passed around, I asked Marvin whether he was aware that this little meal contained liver. He replied that he was, and that he loved liver.

I did not share Marvin's enthusiasm. During the 1930s depression years my parents supplemented our meat diet with tripe and animal organs such as kidneys and liver, which in those days were very inexpensive. For some reason, as I grew older I developed a dislike for these things. I remember expressing my dislike as a young man by telling my brains-eating friends the rather gross joke about a man who, when served with a plate of brains asked 'Are these brains fresh?' and was told by the waiter,

'They certainly are; they were thinking only an hour ago.'

Over the intervening years, my dislike of these animal organs had grown into a revulsion; so while Marvin ate the bits of liver scattered randomly along his skewer with undisguised delight I was wondering how I could locate and avoid eating the bits on mine without upsetting our hosts.

I finally hit on a way of doing it. I would tear off a little piece of *ekmek* and fold it around the piece of meat at the top of my skewer. Then I would pull the meat off in its little *ekmek* cover (this, incidentally, was the accepted way of eating shishkebab in Turkey). As I held this 'mini-sandwich' to my mouth I would smell it to determine whether it was normal goat meat or liver. If it was not liver, I would eat the lot. But if it was, I would surreptitiously let the meat fall to the ground and eat only the *ekmek*.

I'm not sure that any of this tedious process was worth the trouble—particularly since the remaining goat flesh was the toughest meat I'd ever had in my mouth. I could manage only a couple of rubbery pieces, and when I thought no one was watching I tossed the remaining pieces over my shoulder into the bushes.

When everyone had finished eating, and we were drinking our

çay, I noticed that the goat had been dismembered and was being salted and packed away in calico bags for later use.

Plans to move out were now underway. The fire had been extinguished and was about to be buried. All tell-tale signs of our having camped there were being systematically removed. I looked down the valley. Just above the horizon between the trees, the first light of dawn was appearing.

We were about to enter our second day as hostages. It was over thirty hours since we had been captured. This was Sunday. In Australia it would now be around midday.

Had news of our kidnapping been received there yet? If it had been, then our families would be experiencing not only the initial shock of learning that we had been abducted, but also the stresses of knowing so little and imagining so much. Realising that I was powerless to let them know we were alive and safe, I took a moment to pray that our wives and families would be given strength to cope.

Once more, guns were checked and loaded. Once more the metallic clicks of the procedure had the same unnerving effect on me. The order to move out was given. As the column formed up, I found myself behind the guard who was leading us. We went straight up the side of the valley, then ascended a spur which would take us to the top of the nearby mountain range.

It was broad daylight when we reached a point just below the summit. After pausing there for a minute or so, the guard in front of me slipped his gun around on its shoulder-strap into the horizontal alert position. He beckoned me into a spot close behind him then began to climb upwards with myself, and a little further back the rest of the group, following.

This part of the mountaintop was broad and flat. Visibility was reduced to about ten or fifteen feet by a cover of thick bushes and small trees. My guard gave me the signal to stay close behind him, then began to weave his way across the area. As we moved between trees and bushes we pushed their branches aside with the utmost care. We were also careful not to step on any of the broken twigs which littered the whole area.

When he came to a clearing, my guard did not attempt to cross it. He stood there quite still looking straight ahead, then held up his left hand as a traffic policeman might do. We both stood there motionless. When he was satisfied that it was safe to cross, he gave a quick 'move on' signal, again without looking back, and darted across the open ground with me in pursuit.

It was perfectly obvious to me, as I followed him through the undergrowth, that he believed there could be Turkish soldiers here on this mountain. Certainly they could have been deposited by one of the many helicopters flying around the area the day before.

It was also obvious that this young guard was in full battle mode. When we came to a kind of pathway between the trees he stood there in a slightly stooped position ready to open fire. His stance was not unfamiliar to me. As a young lad brought up in the Australian outback I had hunted rabbits, kangaroos and foxes in country much like this.

This man with me was stalking. I knew that if a Turkish soldier were to come along this track, my guard would almost certainly shoot him. I also knew that if a Turkish soldier were to challenge my guard, he would very probably grab me and use me as a human shield to protect himself.

Perhaps the major danger, however, was that of being seen first and cut down by a burst of machine-gun fire; a very likely possibility at close range in such thick scrub. I was not comforted by the fact that I was wearing a khaki jacket just like the one being worn by my guard. I could only hope that any Turkish soldier we might encounter would be under strict orders not to put any hostage at risk. Such orders of course can be quickly overridden by the emotion of the moment. The self-survival instinct is very strong as is a soldier's training to kill his enemy on sight—particularly if that enemy is a guerrilla who might have killed one of one's army mates, a friend or a relative.

Once again I found myself hoping that our Turkish military rescuers were not on this mountain and would not attempt to take us from our captors, though the fact that this dilemma was causing me to think this way about soldiers who were risking their lives to save us disturbed me.

The little track we had been watching was still empty. My guard, after a quick glance in both directions, ran across to the cover of the trees on the other side. Once there, he turned, looked both ways again, then signalled me to cross immediately.

As I followed my guard I began to think that this was one mountain where the search party looking for us had not yet placed soldiers. We had not encountered anyone here, nor had we heard any sounds to indicate that the rest of the group had been involved in a military encounter. It seemed, at this point, that we had the mountain to ourselves.

Within ten minutes we had left the summit and were heading down the other side of the mountain. The trees were taller here and their foliage provided quite a dense cover.

After sending and receiving some bird-call signals, my guard moved to a place on the slope where other members of the group were already beginning to congregate. This was to be the spot for our next camp-site.

The guerrillas, as before, sent us downhill from where they were camped. Guards were placed near us and at various points on and around the mountain. We were made to lie down in a little area where the tree foliage was thick enough to screen us off from planes and helicopters. Although it was still quite early in the morning, we soon found ourselves dropping off to sleep. Our body-clocks were beginning to adjust to guerrilla standard time.

Guerrilla fighters are essentially nocturnal. They strike by night and hide by day. It is by their night-time activities that they seek to undermine existing law and order and gain control.

I remember hearing a somewhat propagandist saying on this subject that is occasionally quoted by locals in Eastern Turkey. In English, it takes the form of a little rhyming couplet:

> The army controls the land by day;
> But the night belongs to the PKK.

I had been asleep for only a short time when I was awakened by the sound of a helicopter. I could not see it, but knew that it must be fairly close to our mountain.

Had any of us been spotted? Was this helicopter near the mountain-top over which we had just passed? Was it about to set down soldiers on one of the clearings there? If it did, then any subsequent movement would almost certainly bring them into military contact with us. However, as far as I could see, none of our captors seemed unduly worried by the presence of this helicopter or the threat it posed.

After a few minutes, the noise began to decrease. It was moving away at last. I was relieved, as we all were, that the threat of a confrontation had been withdrawn, if only temporarily. Our relief, however, was to be short-lived. In a matter of minutes another helicopter passed overhead; the first of many that would hover and fly over us at various times throughout the entire day.

Gradually we all became accustomed to the situation. Sometimes we talked together. Sometimes for short periods we even managed to get some sleep.

Our midday meal consisted of *ekmek*, tomato and cucumber, followed by *çay*.

As we ate, I talked with Gary. When I asked how his foot was, he told me it was healing quite nicely. It was only then that I noticed he was no longer wearing his sandals, but had on a pair of brown rubber-soled shoes—the kind worn by all the guerrillas.

'Where did you get those, Gary?' I asked.

'One of the guerrillas gave me his pair,' he replied.

'That was kind of him.'

'Yes, wasn't it?' Gary answered, 'It makes walking so much easier for me.'

'How do they fit?' I asked.

'Perfectly,' he said, with a bargain-basement smile.

Knowing that guerrillas on the march (and hostages too) cannot do without shoes, I could only assume that our captors had an extra pair or two stashed away in one of their haversacks. Perhaps if I behaved myself I might be next in line for a pair.

While we were relaxing after our meal, the man in charge, who had shared his political views by the camp-fire the previous night, came over to talk with us. He sat down cross-legged in our little group, lit up a cigarette and then began to initiate a conversation. The first phase of this conversation was friendly, but because of the enormous language gap between us, painfully difficult and slow. Several times there seemed no way to bridge that gap. He would say something in Kurdish and then from the expression, or lack of it, on our faces would realise that we hadn't understood; whereupon he would employ a range of explanatory gestures and mime.

Any one of us who thought he had understood would then have to find a way of conveying that understanding back to him without the benefit of language.

It was all like a crazy game of charades, in which nobody had any way of knowing whether he had correctly identified what had been mimed except by miming it back to the mimer.

Understandably, the first phase of the conversation was a dismal failure. However, one benefit emerged from this linguistic deadlock. Our Kurdish host realised that he would have to loosen up considerably on his policy of not conversing in Turkish. This made the situation easier for us, since collectively a few of us knew enough basic Turkish to make ourselves understood to some extent. In addition to this, Gary had a Turkish-English dictionary in his mini-haversack. So in the second phase of our conversation we launched into Turkish, passing the dictionary back and forth to elicit and clarify meanings.

Predictably it was not long before our host began to use this improved means of communication for PKK political purposes.

As in our earlier camp-fire discussion, the major theme was the oppressive injustice of Turkish rule and the evils of Western imperialism, particularly as exemplified in American government policies. This theme was repeated several times. Each time he made his point, we nodded to show that we understood. However, a young guard who was standing nearby and following all this, misinterpreted our nods as expressions of political endorsement. He leaned towards us and with a beaming smile said,

'Karl Marx, *tammum*? Karl Marx, *tammum*, eh?'

Being advocates of free enterprise and Western democracy, none of us was keen to discuss the political merits of Karl Marx with this zealous young man. So we sat there and said nothing.

As the discussion proceeded, the soft-voiced man who had killed and butchered the goat the night before joined our little group. He did not speak to us directly but from time to time, without looking up, exchanged private comments with the older man who sat next to him. His voice was calm, quiet and satin-smooth. His every word was measured and deliberate, as though planned carefully beforehand. Just as he knew the anatomy of the goat he had slaughtered, so too he knew the anatomy of each of his sentences before he laid it bare. It seemed to me that this cerebral young man was no ordinary guerrilla. Whatever he was, it was not for his butchering expertise that he was attached to the group. Although he did not exercise command over the group, he spoke as an equal to the man who did. I suspected that within the military hierarchy of the PKK he was a high-ranking officer of some kind.

Our discussion with the man in charge had been going on for well over an hour when it entered its third phase. He took from his pocket a blank plastic-bound book. It was about the size of a small desk-diary, but not as thick. It was dog-eared, soiled and bent from being carried in his army jacket. He opened it, turned it upside down then handed it across for us to peruse. The first page contained personal details about the owner, including his name—Ibrahim. The rest of the book contained photographs. The first half featured Ibraham, his family and friends; but as we turned the pages, I noticed that the family pictures of the earlier section gave way to group shots of guerrillas. As we looked at them he pointed certain people out to us and explained that many of them had been killed.

When we had finished looking through the book, he took it back and began to thumb through it. He was silent as he tenderly turned each page. He stopped at one in particular and, with his fist just under his nose, looked intently at it. Then wiping a knuckle quickly across the corner of one eye, he closed the book and slipped it back into his inside pocket.

Suddenly his mood changed. He asked Marvin and Richard whether they would like him to take a picture of them. Before they could say yes or no, they found themselves being posed for a typical guerrilla group shot. They were handed the heavy machine-gun which the group carried everywhere with them complete with its tripod stand. The huge ammunition belt that feeds bullets into it was hung, like a python in a circus act, around Marvin's neck.

A little red warning-light flashed on in the back of my mind. Such a photograph could subsequently be used to show that we were willing to be identified with PKK weaponry and by implication PKK methods and ideology. It would in fact brand us as collaborators.

The thought that such a picture might end up under clear plastic in Ibrahim's little album was disturbing enough. But I went weak at the knees when I realised that it might find its way into PKK publicity files and from there be sent on to newspapers who would publish it with misleading captions on the front page.

Casting aside all discretion, I began to blurt out my warning not to be photographed in this compromising pose. I had hardly said half a sentence when, to my relief, the gun was handed back and Marvin had divested himself of the ammunition belt. The photograph was not taken. We had handed in our weapons and mercifully had not been 'shot'. Blessed are the peacemakers.

Had we offended Ibrahim? Not in the slightest, it seemed. With a smiling *'Tammum,'* he shrugged his shoulders, stood up and left us, thus bringing this incident and phase three of our conversation with him to a close.

The long conversation and the heat of the afternoon had tired us out. In the lengthening shadows, we all began to relax.

I leaned back against a tree and looked out over the mountain range which extended right to the horizon. Its light green forest cover was now mellowing in the afternoon sunlight. There was no sound; not a bird call, not even the hum of an insect. This was generally the way it was here in the mountains of Eastern Turkey—even at sunrise, when one expects to hear such sounds.

How different it was to the Australian bush! Mountains like these would be alive with the calls of birds as they fluttered about in trees and swooped by, often in large flocks. Even in our deserts, little sparrows and finches constantly flit about in the low mulga scrub and bushes. And on a hot day like this one, there would almost always be two other sounds; one the mournful wail of the black crow and the other (as anyone who has cooked meat on a camp-fire would know) the buzz of huge blowflies.

I was not the least bit nostalgic about the blowflies. But at that moment, my spirits would have been lifted by some Australian bird sounds; the raucous chuckle of a kookaburra, the chirp of a rosella parrot...or even the plaintive cry of an old man crow.

My eyes roamed out to the mountains on my left. Somewhere out there, I thought, was the place where we had been kidnapped. The mountains in that area had probably been thoroughly combed by now—and I was sure that both the ground and air search-parties would be radiating out from it further and further as time progressed. I could imagine those in charge of the operation having in their headquarters maps on which concentric circles would by now have been drawn, to indicate how far we could have travelled in so many days. The presence of such a large number of helicopters in the area suggested to me that the

Turkish authorities strongly suspected, or actually knew, that we were hiding here somewhere.

Even if those searching for us did know that we were here, the problem of rescuing us alive posed a formidable problem. How could they get us away from our captors—who, if they wanted to, could shoot us all the moment they tried?

As much as I was aware that this could happen, it seemed to me that the last thing these guerrillas wanted was for us to be killed or even harmed. To be involved in anything like that would be to portray themselves as brutal thugs rather than fair-minded advocates of a responsibly governed Kurdistan. Nonetheless a shoot-out could not be discounted—especially if the Turkish military encircled us and pinned us all down here on this mountain without water or food. I thought that our captors would move out before such a stand-off situation could develop and then escalate, and that they'd probably do it under cover of darkness tonight.

I could hear them preparing our evening meal. As this was being done they allowed us to borrow their radio again. While Marvin was exploring the shortwave band, he came across a BBC news bulletin, this time in English. One of the news items described what had happened to us in considerable detail. While it did not give our names, it did correctly describe our nationalities: three Americans, one Briton and one Australian. It went on to say that the Turkish Government had authorised a massive search for us involving some 4,000 soldiers. It also added (incorrectly, in Gary's case) that we had come to Turkey for the purpose of excavating a site where Noah's ark was thought to be buried. This bulletin indicated not only that our kidnapping was still world news but that the search for us was more massive than anything we could have imagined. We also knew from this broadcast that the information about our archaeological project could only have been gained from Ron's or my wife. Our families would certainly have known about us by now.

After we had eaten our evening meal, which on this occasion was supplemented by cold goat meat, we heard for the first time (but did not see) a little ritual for all of the guerrillas in the group except our guards. It seemed to involve a short lecture of some kind, followed by a number of chorused responses to a familiar pattern of questions recited by the leader. Of course we did not know what was being said, because it was all in Kurdish. However, it was clear that it was some kind of morale-building exercise to heighten commitment to the PKK cause. As soon as the ritual was finished the group went through the usual processes of breaking camp and moving out.

Night had not yet fallen as our column made its way back to the summit of the mountain.

In which direction would they take us now? Their options seemed limited. They would certainly not be able to take us back to the region where we had been kidnapped. Nor could they safely head into the nearby mountain area which now could be full of troops set down by helicopters. To go back to the wide valley through which we had marched the previous night would be to risk meeting army vehicles, now probably patrolling the road there.

It was clear that in this part of the mountains there was nowhere to hide any more. As far as I could see, the only place for us to go would be to a range of mountains visible in the distance, largely denuded of trees and glowing amber-brown in the last rays of the setting sun.

The column began to move in its direction. To get there would involve a trek of many hours. Much of it would involve hard climbing, too; first to get down off the present range which was steep and quite heavily timbered on this side, and then to get up on to those other mountains.

I wondered whether we'd have the stamina to make it in one night's journey. My main concern, though, was for Ron. I was not sure that he was yet able to move on.

As we began to slide and slither our way down the mountain slope between the trees, I looked across the vast expanse of flat land between this range and the other. There would be virtually nowhere for us to hide as we made our way across. This was going to be a very risky journey. However, our captors had one thing in their favour. Should any of those 4,000 Turkish soldiers who were out looking for us intercept them, their chances of survival would be much better because we were marching along with them.

And what were our chances of survival right now? Hopefully, about as good as theirs.

Whether we liked it or not, we were now bound together, captor and captive cheek by jowl, with the cords of mutual dependency. These cords were chafing and drawing tight.

CHAPTER

5

Who Is The Enemy?

O ur mountain descent was difficult. After some forty tedious
minutes on the slopes, I began to feel the symptoms of 'jelly
leg'.

I looked back and saw that Ron was again being supported by
two guerrillas, one on either side of him. When we made our first
stop, I asked him how he was managing.

'I'm doing fine,' he gasped, 'but I don't know how these two
guerrillas would have made it down the mountain if I hadn't
carried them.'

I was directly behind the leader. He was setting a cracking
pace as he almost jogged down over the gravelly slopes. Several
times he briefly paused, surveyed the next section of the descent,
then, signalling me to follow, quietly hurried on.

On one occasion, my saddle-booted feet slipped from under
me. I thumped down heavily on to my backside and slid noisily
down the slope. I could feel the sharp burning sensation of the
gravel as it scraped my skin through the thin material of my
boiler suit. I envisaged an impressive mottled-blue bruise, nicely
decorated with striations of parallel red grazes.

My guard stopped and turned round. Looking at me with a
frown, he shook his head with a 'tch-tch-tch', as though berating
a foolish child.

I was quickly up again, on my way and moving down the last
little incline. I could hear the rest of the group sliding down over
the gravel behind me.

Another ten minutes saw our column tramping across wide flat terrain towards the distant range, now barely visible in the dark distance of the night.

It promised to be a long hard march. As we tramped along, my mind began to wander back over what had happened during the last couple of days. I realised that we five were experiencing things that few Westerners have ever experienced. Hostages are rarely made to do what we were doing. They are usually hidden away by their kidnappers—incarcerated in some remote place, often in solitary confinement with little or no knowledge even of their captors.

But for the five of us it was different. Everywhere our captors went, we went. Where they hid, we hid. What they ate, we ate. We lived basically as they lived. Ours was a cheek-by-jowl experience of guerrilla life on the run.

If we should survive it, then our account of what had happened to us would be stamped with an immediacy that comes only from genuine first-hand experience.

I could not help remembering, as we trudged mechanically along, how certain historical works have this characteristic—the mark of personal experience, that authentic quality that comes from being an on-the-spot observer.

Many events of the Bible are of this kind. The Gospels are well-known examples of this.[1] The Old Testament is also replete with evidences of it,[2] the account of the flood in Genesis 6–8 being a particularly interesting example.

As we marched on, I remembered the work of Wing Commander P.J. Wiseman, RAF, who wrote a book showing that Genesis was written by men who were actual eye-witnesses to the events they described. This book, *New Discoveries in Babylonia About Genesis*[3], had greatly impressed me. The author, a very experienced Middle-Eastern archaeological researcher, had brought forward strong evidence to show that within the Genesis text itself there were acknowledgements of the various authors who had contributed their respective segments of the record.

Wiseman, from his extensive study of Babylonian clay tablets, had realised that the oft-repeated phrase 'these are the generations of...' was, in numerous instances, a form of historical documentation identifying the writer of the foregoing account.[4]

In much the same way that we sign a document or a letter to

indicate that we have written it and that it is a true account, so too, each of the writers of Genesis 'signed off' his particular section. Hence, the phrase, 'these are the generations of Noah', means essentially, 'these [that is, the things I have just written] are the historical facts [the history or account] "generated" or "brought into being" by Noah'.[5]

While the Hebrew word *tolêdâh* translated 'generation' is often followed in Genesis by genealogical data, Wiseman points out that in the instances he cites, which include those of the flood account, it could also mean a 'history' or an 'account' written by the person or persons named. On this basis, the first part of the flood account (Gen 6:1-9) could in fact have been penned by Noah himself,[6] and the second part (Gen 6:10–10:1) by the sons of Noah, Shem, Ham and Japheth.[7]

As I thought all this over, I could not help but be impressed once again by the fact that if Wiseman was right, Moses, the compiler of Genesis, Exodus, Leviticus, Numbers and Deuteronomy, had fulfilled well his editorial responsibilities by preserving with these accounts the names of those who had penned them.[8] If Wiseman's theory was correct, then those who had set down the events associated with the Flood and the ark were literally eyewitnesses to them. And if this were the case, then little wonder, I thought, that there was such a large amount of highly specific detail there.

Historians engaged in archaeological research are usually delighted when first-hand accounts come into their hands. Such accounts often provide them with just the kind of checklist detail they need to locate and identify what they are looking for.[9]

How interesting it would be, I thought, to see whether the very detailed Genesis account from which a number of us were working would be archaeologically confirmed as an accurate firsthand account of the kind P.J. Wiseman claimed it was.

I was grateful to have had the opportunity to be an eye-witness myself to so many of the things which I had previously only read about or seen in pictures and video tapes. The quite vast array of information which comes from actually being there puts things into a balance and a context that do not come in any other way. The eye and the hand pick things up and prompt questions which are never even asked unless one is a first-hand witness.

I thought back to the controversial anchor or drogue stones

most of which I had now been privileged to examine personally several times. I recalled how these drogue stones had been written off by a host of people who had never even examined them or seriously considered the now quite substantial amount of information about them.[10]

I felt that even a brief, personal visit to this particular site would throw considerable doubt on some of the claims that these huge slabs of rock with their brilliantly hollowed-out holes were not drogue stones.[11]

Just a few years ago, for example, two more stones were found buried nearby. However, these stones, unlike the others, are not decorated in any way. They have no crosses or decorations of any kind and there is no reason to suppose that they had ever been stood up vertically as the tombstones in the area are. They are probably exactly what they look like; huge stones that show us what the others looked like before they were erected and decorated to commemorate some past event.[12]

Further proof that these stones near Arzap are not tombstones with holes in them is readily available to anyone who takes the trouble to examine yet another of these stones (as members of our team have done) which is lying on a mountain a few miles away and is nowhere near a cemetery.[13]

Like the majority of the Arzap stones, this one has also been decorated, but there is nothing to suggest that it is or ever was a gravestone.

When I was examining these objects with Jack Bouma the engineer and architect, I watched him run his hands over them. He said to me, 'These stones have been smoothed by the kind of abrasion that might occur if they were dragged over a rocky surface'—which is, of course, exactly what can happen to drogue stones.

Some have said that these stones cannot be drogues because the holes in them are too high and that the tops would break off if they were raised on ropes.[14] There were two factors which would militate against this happening. The first was that the hole is bored through the thickest part of the drogue stone (a fact not apparent in most photographs but readily so to the on-site observer). The second is that drogues are designed for the buoyant environment of water, not air. Those who designed them placed each hole high enough to enable the stone's hydrodynamic function to be served without risking breakage. All these stones are essentially the same in basic structure. All have been hewn into a similar shape. All have the same kind of holes cleverly hollowed out near the tops, as if designed to hold a knotted rope in such a way that it would not slip out.[15]

All of these characteristics tend to lead one to the conclusion that the objects are anchors or drogues.

The fact that they are all essentially the same in design and yet not all decorated and not all standing in a cemetery would seem to preclude their being tombstones of any kind. The decorations on a number of these stones, although highly interesting, do *not* change the possibility that they are drogue stones—decorated for some reason with various kinds of ancient crosses, but possibly drogue stones nonetheless.

Until compelling evidence to the contrary emerges, it would seem prudent to assume that these dozen or more stones found within 10–15 miles of the boat-shaped formation may be what the on-site evidence strongly indicates they are—drogue stones. The possibility that they have been decorated with ancient pre-Christian and/or post-Christian era crosses to memorialise some important event, with which the stones themselves may have been associated, needs to be seriously considered.

Furthermore, the fact that they are so much larger than other drogue stones yet located raises the possibility that they might somehow be associated with one of the largest vessels known to the ancient world.[16]

Although there is much for historians to learn from written documents and various other records, some of the most important information comes from personal contact, discussions and interviews with local people. Many of these people know things which have never been written or published. And some of these things can be of vital importance to a project of this kind. My mind ran back over the personal interviews I had only recently completed with three local men who claimed to have been in the Akyayla area when the boat-shaped formation was supposed to have emerged as a result of an earthquake in 1948.[17] David Fasold had interviewed a local man called Reshit a few years earlier concerning this occurrence. The interview had yielded some important information[18] and I was anxious to supplement it by further interviews, if possible with Reshit and others.

To this end, I had made arrangements to interview three local men who claimed to be eye-witnesses to the earthquake which possibly occurred in 1948. The men were Hasan Ozer, Ismail Sarihan and Reshit Sarihan. In 1948 all three lived in the area. Hasan Ozer being 51 years of age would have been a child of about eight at that time. Both Ismail Sarihan and Reshit Sarihan were seventy-five years old now and therefore would have been young men of around thirty-two years of age in that year.

I carefully formulated a series of questions that were asked of each man in Kurdish. None of the men interviewed was aware of the questions I was planning to ask beforehand. None of them when invited to be interviewed had any opportunity to discuss the subject with the others. Each was interviewed separately.[19]

All three gave the following five pieces of information:

- Prior to the earthquake there was no sign of the boat-shaped formation in the valley where it now stands. All that existed there was a field or fields where grass was cut for animals.

- Prior to the earthquake and the appearance of the formation, the field used to slip slowly down the valley (the sloping valley floor is a mud-slip area).

- When the earthquake occurred, many rocks or stones came down the slope and over the fields.

- As these stones came down, the formation began to come up, but not all at once. It didn't happen in one day, but emerged slowly day by day.

- Although the rocks or stones continued to come down the slope, the formation did not move but continued to stand there (all three found it strange that the formation did not move).

None of the men gave a specific date for the earthquake that resulted in the formation's appearance, although they were all aware that it was around the late 1940s and 1950s. They all commented on the fact that there had been several earthquakes in the area.

The information yielded by these interviews confirmed in general terms the responses by Reshit Sarihan in the interview conducted by David Fasold a few years earlier.[20]

The general consensus on the major events described in the interviews tends to confirm their authenticity. There were also other pieces of information volunteered by at least two of the men which lent further authenticity and credibility to their testimonies. All three, for example, referred to the village's being endangered by the rocks which came down the mountain. All three made reference to the fact that the changes in the valley terrain brought by the earthquake took away their fields—a serious matter for those whose livelihood depended upon the availability of this land. Two of them told of dwellings which at that time were near the place where the boat-shaped formation appeared. Both quite independently gave the names of those who lived in these dwellings. There were also other pieces of information about who came to the site, what they did and what they found there, which tallied with well-established information we already had.

It seemed to me from this information and from the manner in which it was shared that these men were describing real events. Their testimonies provided, I thought, a reasonable basis for the belief that before this earthquake, the large boat-shaped formation was neither visible nor known to them until it began to emerge at the time of the earthquake.

This evidence, when taken together with that from other sources, enabled us to suggest some tentative ideas about the formation and how it had come to be where it was.

Beginning with Flavius Josephus's reference to Berosus's account,[21] it could be suggested that the place where the ark finally landed and which was later visited by pilgrims was somewhere on this mountain range, perhaps at the altitude where the Akyayla formation exists or perhaps higher up the valley. If it was at a higher location before the Christian era began, which is when Berosus makes reference to it,[22] then it must have moved down from there at a later time. Josephus, in the century following the time of Christ, wrote that the remains of the ark were still there in his own day.[23]

Unfortunately, he did not indicate whether it was higher than the elevation where the Akyayla formation now lay. However the distortion of the western wall, along with other indications of collision and lateral impact, suggested that the formation might have been transported from higher up the valley (a possibility suggested by a number of researchers who have examined it)[24]. It appears to have been arrested in its downward path by the rocky outcrop which impaled it and was eventually covered by mud from higher up the slope.

Thus it might have been hidden from view for many centuries; until in 1948 an earthquake brought it to the surface, and subsequent earth movement and erosion gradually caused its present appearance.

From the many pieces of evidence available to us, it seemed feasible to summarise a possible order of events based on the hypothetical assumption that the boat-shaped Akyayla formation is the ark. For many centuries after the flood the vessel had remained somewhere on the western slope of the mountain, most probably at a higher elevation than where it sits now. It was observed and visited there more than two centuries before Christ. It is possible that it might have remained there until well into the first century after Christ. However, it was later transported by some kind of earth movement to the place where it rests now. At some time following this, it was totally covered by mud and probably remained so until the mid-twentieth century when (very possibly in 1948) it became visible again following an earthquake.

Was this an accurate log of the ark's final journey? Did this vessel, long after Noah and the rest of its occupants had disembarked, ride the Akyayla mud rapids down the valley to be wrecked on the rocky reef that holds it fast to this very day?

This possible order of events was not inconsistent with the documented accounts in our possession.[25] I had cause to be grateful to all those Middle-Eastern men who, down through the centuries, had been willing to go on record with eye-witness information about these matters.

Except for the few times when we waited briefly to give and receive reconnaissance signals, the entire journey was completed in one gruelling five-hour push. To my great relief we were not intercepted. Nor was there any indication that we had even been observed.

When we arrived parched and weary at the foothills of the range, we turned left and followed them until we reached the entrance to a wide valley. As we turned into it, I couldn't help wondering whether the Turkish troops were already emplaced here and watching us from the mountains on either side.

After another hour of brisk trekking, the leader of the group signalled us to stop, made a cricket-chirping sound and waited for it to be returned.

I noticed, as we stood there in the cool stillness of the evening, that Ron and the two men helping him along were not with us. They showed up a couple of minutes later, just as we were about to move out. Poor Ron! He did not get the benefit of even the small respite we'd had.

As we trudged on, the gradient of the valley floor increased. Although it could not yet be described as steep, my body was beginning to show some of the early symptoms of exhaustion. I was finding it hard to lift my legs and my breathing was becoming laboured. Apart from a few small stops, we had been marching, without food or water, for almost seven hours. The guerrillas were obviously trying to put as much distance between us and our pursuers as they could. They probably thought that by doing this they could exceed Turkish military estimates of how far we could have travelled.

The gradient continued to steepen as we pressed on towards the head of the valley. I was finding it difficult to continue as I summoned the concentration to take each separate step. I sensed I was nearing my physical limit. I could hear the others gasping for each breath too as they sought to gulp down enough air to oxygenate their rapidly enervating bodies. I knew that if our captors forced us to climb this steepening slope much longer, my body would stubbornly refuse to obey the orders issued to it by my tired mind.

I glanced back. Ron and his two guards were nowhere to be seen. I was worried that he might have already reached the point of physical collapse which I was rapidly approaching. Was he lying on the ground unconscious, as he had been three nights ago? Was he dangerously ill, or even worse?

There seemed to be nothing any of us could do but pray that Ron and the rest of us would, by God's grace, not break under this mounting pressure.

Somehow, I managed to gather just enough strength to put forward one leaden foot after the other.

The dryness of my mouth and throat together with my

increased temperature indicated that I was becoming dehydrated. I knew that these guerrillas, like the Australian aborigines, did not normally carry water with them on a journey. Water is very heavy and carrying it over long distances can seriously deplete energy reserves. These men were heading for some mountain retreat where there was a stream, as well as a forest, in which to hide. Until we reached that place, there would be no water and no rest for any of us. I was wondering how much further on this spot would be, when I heard the trickle of water. The welcome sound came from a little gully only a few yards away.

The column was halted and we were soon scooping up and drinking handfuls of cool water from a shallow pool.

This was the first time I had ever drunk a substantial amount of water directly from a natural stream anywhere in Turkey. Of course, the water we had been given since our capture had all come from such streams and we had accepted it because there was simply no alternative. The fact that we had imbibed virtually all of it as tea which had been boiled beforehand had allayed most of our concerns.

However, as I knelt by this little watercourse and swallowed its cooling contents, the tourist bureau warnings of 'Never drink the water', leaped to my mind.

I had good reason to recall this warning. On my first visit to Turkey I had scrupulously observed this safeguard by drinking only commercially purified water which I carried with me in a bottle wherever I travelled. Consequently, by the time I was ready to return home I was feeling quite pleased with myself for having avoided all the stomach upsets that can turn a visit to Turkey into a misery. Little did I realise, as I ate my final hotel meal before flying out of the country, that Turkey, like the scorpion with the sting in its tail, had a nasty little farewell nip for me. The waiter brought me a jug of iced water which normally would have been purified and in this instance probably was. However, the ice in it probably wasn't.

I had swallowed only one mouthful when my stomach began to churn. The experience of enduring thirty-three hours of jet travel with griping stomach pains and nausea is one I shall not easily forget.

However, the memory of the mountain water and its restorative effect refreshes me still. No beverage, however exotic or expensive, will ever compare with the plain water I drank from that little stream.

The temptation to drink too much of it was difficult to resist. However, I contented myself with eight or nine mouthfuls, knowing that a greater quantity could cause stomach cramps, especially if there was more strenuous climbing ahead; and there was little doubt of that. They would not camp in this exposed location, but would continue up the valley to some hideaway in the mountains or even beyond them.

Neither Ron nor his helpers was anywhere to be seen.

By now, everyone in the group, including Richard, Gary and Marvin, had quenched their thirst. Most of them were lying on a narrow little slope that ran parallel to the stream. Some were already asleep. Marvin was one of these. In Australia, we say that sound sleepers like Marvin 'could sleep on a barbed-wire fence'. As I lay down next to him, I noticed he was comfortably curled up on his side, both knees together, his head pillowed on his bent arm; his deep relaxed breathing about to become a robust snore.

Although the water had cooled my mouth and throat, my body temperature was still uncomfortably high. The unyielding and uncomfortable ground beneath me felt cold and soothing to my hot tired muscles. I was almost asleep when I heard the sound of approaching footsteps.

Ron and his guards had caught up with us at last. As they approached the stream, Ron's forearms dangled loosely over the chests of the two men supporting him. His florid face, heavy-lidded eyes and loosely-hanging jaw all indicated a state of near collapse. In a few minutes he had slaked his thirst, was lying down nearby and along with the rest of us had fallen into an exhausted sleep.

Barely forty minutes later we were awakened and formed up again into single file. As I stood up I realised that the cool of the ground that had soothed me earlier had penetrated deeply into my muscles and bones while I was asleep. I was now stiff and aching with cold.

As we continued our ascent through the narrowing valley, we followed the creek. Its waters meandered through little hollows and trenches which it had incised for itself in the clay of the valley floor. We crossed back and forth over these as we climbed higher.

When the creek-bed deepened into a steep-sided gorge, we had to leave it and make our way up the side of the valley along a narrow ridge. The ascent was slow and arduous. After half an hour of hard climbing over rocks and around massive boulders, we were given permission to take a brief rest.

I lowered myself to the ground and leaned against a large boulder. Its coldness chilled the overheated muscles of my back, as an ice-pack might do. I closed my eyes and breathed deeply. My body began to relax. But within two minutes, an order from the leader had us all on our feet and in line, ready to leave.

I looked down the valley and there was Ron again, his feet almost dragging between the two men supporting him. I was afraid it would be just as it had been earlier in the evening. They would catch up with us just as we were leaving and force Ron to go on with us—without giving him any opportunity to rest.

As they climbed up towards us, I broke ranks without permission and went down to meet them.

I spoke directly to Ron as I laid my hand on his shoulder.

'Have a rest, Ron. Sit down.'

'I'll be OK,' he breathed faintly.

'Not if you don't rest,' I said. There was an edge of anger to my voice.

The two guerrillas, their own strength now considerably depleted, ducked their heads and lifted Ron's arms from off their shoulders.

His knees buckled as he sank to the ground. Ron knew that the group was about to leave; he would not allow himself to lie down and relax. Instead he leaned back on his elbows, his chin on his heaving chest.

'I can make it,' he said.

'It's no good!' I answered roughly, speaking, by the tone of my voice, as much to the guards as to him.

'You can't go on without a break, Ron! We've all had one!'

'Rest up, Ron!' interjected Marvin, just as firmly.

'We're not moving on', I protested angrily, 'until you've had a break.'

Then suiting action to word, I sat down next to him, my arms around my knees and my hands gripped tight; as street protesters sometimes do when told to move on by the police.

I waited for the sharp metallic prod of a gun barrel.

It did not come.

Our guards stayed with us and the rest of the group went on.

I looked down the valley and out to those village lights, now barely visible. I thanked God that we had been able to stand our ground on this important little issue and, somehow, had got away with it.

In another ten minutes we were on our way again. Ron and his two guards began to drop back and were soon out of sight, hidden behind the boulders which almost blocked this upper part of the valley. When we stopped again, we sat down and waited for them to join us. After a few minutes Ron appeared. He had broken away from the two men who were helping him and was scrambling up on all fours over the rocks that were strewn beside the wall of the valley.

We called out to him to rest, but he would not hear of it. He would stand up unsteadily, then almost lunge forward to gain the momentum he needed to go higher. Eventually he stopped and we persuaded him to rest with us before pressing on again.

The steepest part of the climb was still ahead of us. However, the head of the valley could now be seen towering above us with only the night sky beyond.

Another quarter of an hour and we were there. Most of the guerrillas who had arrived before us were sitting or lying down between the rocks. Some were asleep. The rest of us, wobbly-legged and panting, wearily dropped down beside them.

'Where to now?' I asked myself.

We were on top of a bare rocky mountain pass. On one side, the terrain rose steeply towards the summit of the range. I did not think our captors would take us up that way since there seemed to be no tree-cover to hide us from Turkish aerial reconnaissance. The other side of the pass dropped away into a dark, yawning valley, its steep bouldered slope covered in jagged loose shale. Most of the mountains around this valley were like the one we were on; steep and treeless. I thought it very unlikely that our captors would take us down there.

Finally, I looked ahead in the opposite direction to that from which we had come. Down the other side of this pass and beyond, all I could see was range upon range of treeless mountaintops in the moonlight.

While we five were recuperating, a few of the guerrillas were conferring. From their gestures, they seemed to be discussing which way to go. I was glad it was their decision and not mine. My only hope was the fervent one that our destination, wherever it was, would not be far away.

Immediately the conference was over they began to line us up. From the direction they made us face, it was soon apparent where they were planning to take us. To our horror, we realised we were about to head straight down over the unstable shale-covered slope of that frightening valley. The descent would be made more hazardous by the fact that everything there was in deep shadow.

I stood back at the rear of the column with Ron. One by one those ahead of us stepped out of the moonlight and down into the darkness. 'They don't know where they are going,' said Ron, struggling to control his anger. 'This whole thing has turned into a nightmare.' As I followed him over the edge I could hardly help but agree.

Every step was fraught with danger. At the touch of a foot, any of those loose fragments of stone could slip from under the climber and send him crashing down on to the boulders below.

'No one in his right mind would tackle this slope, even in broad daylight,' I thought, as I gently tested each treacherous rock with the weight of my next step.

Down below I could see the others; small, shadowy figures each hunched in a sideways stance, tentatively transferring his weight from the bent, up-slope leg to the extended lower one.

How relieved I was when my guard and I finally completed that dangerous dark descent! As we stepped down into the moon-lit foothills, I marvelled that none of us had been injured on the way down.

Our column went down between the giant boulders that littered the lower slopes of the valley. Why had they brought us down here? There were no trees under which to hide. There was no sign of water to drink. Everything on the bottom of this valley appeared to be bare and moistureless.

Once more, due to the exertion to which we had been subjected since our last drink, my tongue was beginning to stick to the roof of my mouth. After tramping on for another half-mile or so, we reached a little creek. To my delight it contained flowing water. Our column for a few moments marched along its bank. Why didn't we all stop and drink from it?

With a mixture of annoyance and dismay, I saw the leader of the column step across the stream and strike out towards the mountains bordering the valley. The rest of the group, without a murmur, followed on.

When it was my turn to cross, I realised that the entire group was moving on without even bothering to fill those empty water containers.

I stepped into the mud of the creek bed and, turning to my guard, pointed down to the water as it gurgled gently by near my feet. '*Su, chok guzel su?*' I said. To my comment that here was water—very good water, he simply responded by waving me brusquely on.

I wondered whether, unknown to me, they had checked the water beforehand and found it polluted. Perhaps they had seen a dead animal upstream. Whatever their reason for not stopping, the subject was closed. We continued to follow the others up another dry valley towards a low ridge dotted with bushes.

When we reached a place just below the top of this ridge, we were told to lie down and rest. I found a piece of stick, used it to scrape out a hip-hole for myself in the gravelly clay, and was soon asleep.

When I awoke it was about four o'clock. I was too stiff and cold to go back to sleep so I stood up and walked around in an effort to warm up. Except for the two men standing guard, everyone else was sound asleep.

I noticed that Ron was beginning to stir. In a minute or so he was fully awake. By now he seemed to be somewhat recovered. We exchanged a few brief comments as we stood in the near-freezing night air with our collars up, our arms crossed over our chests and our hands tucked under our armpits inside our jackets.

I agreed with Ron that our captors seemed to be unfamiliar with the area and probably didn't know where to go next. We also discussed the problem of having no water, and agreed that if they made us trek much further or even endure another hot day without it, we would all be in very serious trouble.

In a little while the guards were changed. One of the men who was going off duty had trouble waking the young man rostered to take his place. He shook him by the shoulder but he did not respond. Even when he was called by name and shaken more roughly, he still did not move. A couple of other guerrillas came to the guard's assistance. But after more persistent prodding and pummelling from all of them, the young man, who was barely sixteen, did not move. I found it difficult to suppress a chuckle. I knew the problem well; one of my own sons was, and occasionally still is, just as unresponsive. It was only after five minutes of shoving and shouting by his comrades that the young lad was roused and up on his feet.

He must surely have been hot favourite for the Guerrilla Sleepstakes. However, as I looked down at Marvin, who was still superbly slumbering, I wasn't so sure.

Two guerrillas gathered up the water containers and headed down towards the stream we had crossed earlier. It was well over half an hour before they returned. By the time we had all quenched our thirst the eastern sky was beginning to lighten. We formed up and headed along the ridge towards the only tree-clad prominence in sight—a steep-sided little mountain barely half a mile away.

When we began to climb it, we found its undergrowth almost impenetrable. Soon we were entangled in a thicket of shrubs; tall springy stems having to be bent or broken off before we could squeeze our way through. Much of the tree foliage was barely head high and sharp-ended broken branches were a constant threat to face and eye.

When we had climbed about half-way up, we were ordered to stop. Our guard told us to sit. The branches and leaves were barely chest-high. We five obediently sat or squatted as best we could on the sharp rocks and knobbly roots which protruded everywhere. The rest of the group went a little higher up the slope to a rock ledge just above us.

Two men, as usual, were left to guard us. They stood nearby, with their heads and shoulders among the leaves. Unsatisfactory as it was, it seemed that this spot was to be our hiding place for the day which was just about to break.

We were all tired and desperately in need of sleep. However, since there was barely enough room to stretch out and virtually nowhere to lie comfortably, all we could manage to do was fitfully doze for the next couple of hours.

After breakfast, the five of us began to discuss our situation.

We decided it was time we talked to Ibrahim about our release. Ibrahim was known to the rest of the group as 'General', so through our guards we asked if the General would come down and talk with us.

After an hour or so he came. Then, aided by the vocabulary from our little Turkish dictionary, we raised the question of our release. He studiously avoided answering and began instead to discuss the subject of how we had been treated as hostages. He asked us whether we had been fed adequately. Knowing that we had eaten just as well as his guerrilla group, we assured him that we had no complaints about food. This appeared to please him. He almost seemed to be suggesting that since we were being fed three meals a day in a country where this was a rarity for many, why should we want to leave? Such an argument had a kind of rough logic to it.

After all, the guerrillas under his command received nothing from the PKK but their daily ration of food, and if they were quite content with that, why shouldn't we be? Furthermore, if his men never raised the subject of going home to their families, why should he be obliged to discuss it with us? He then began to remind us that the Turkish military were the real aggressors and that if he were to hand us over to them, they might shoot us all and then claim that the PKK had done it. He added that by contrast, we were safe here with the PKK.

How clever he was. In spite of his country background, Ibrahim shared with other generals a good grasp of railroad engineering, the skills of which he had just demonstrated by expertly shunting our train of thought into a siding.

When he left us, we discussed the matter further. I expressed the opinion that within their limited capabilities, this group had obviously made an effort to treat us well, hoping no doubt, that we might say so when released. It seemed to me, in fact, that Ibrahim might be rather more willing to release us if he knew that we would not lie about this matter. Though I would never be party to dishonest deals with him, I said that I felt there was no reason why we should not be ready to say, on our release, that we had been given good food and drink and in general treated fairly, if it were true.

Using the vocabulary from our little dictionary, I wrote a short note to this effect in Turkish on the blank fly-leaf.

When Ibrahim càme by again a little later in the morning, I handed it to him. He read it carefully, nodded his head and with a quiet *'Tammum'*, handed it back to me.

When he stood up to leave, I was not sure that this little conversation had been any more productive than the earlier one. We had tried to communicate these matters to him without collaborating with him. How successful we had been in hastening our release remained to be seen.

The day was breezeless and unpleasantly hot. From within our leafy little cavern it was possible to see only a fragmented panorama of the valley and mountains we'd crossed on the previous night. To our right was the mountain pass, its steep, scree-covered slope almost as daunting by day as it had been by night; straight ahead, the opposite side of the valley, its skyline a dramatic combination of brown bluff and ridge; to the left, behind the place where we had briefly slept earlier that morning, more forested mountain slopes; and towering above them, a long, level-summited mountain, burnished brown in the noon-day sun.

Our midday snack was interrupted by the sound of an approaching helicopter.

The strident 'crack-crack-crack' of its exhaust reverberated in our ears as it passed almost directly over us.

'They've finally caught up with us,' I thought, as it headed across the valley towards the ridge on the other side. It hovered there momentarily, then descended behind a bluff and was lost to view.

In a matter of minutes, several other helicopters appeared. They flew across the valley in the same general direction. As they descended behind the mountains, the sound of their engines was muffled, then muted into silence.

Extra guards were sent down the mountainside and the ridge across the valley was scrutinised through powerful binoculars. The entire group was now on full alert.

Marvin, who had excellent long-distance sight, pointed through a space between the leaves.

'Richard,' he said, 'I think I can see movement there on the top of that ridge.'

'So can I,' said Richard. 'They're climbing down into that little dip.'

Ron, Gary and I all peered intently at the ridge. Even with my glasses, I could not see any soldiers there because of my short-sightedness, a legacy of a cataract condition.

What would happen now?

In my mind I began to sift through some of the possibilities.

Although we were very well hidden here, it was just possible that we had now been seen either from the air or from that ridge. If so, plans could already be under way for the Turkish military to move in on our mountain to surround it and cordon it off. However, they might consider this tactic too provocative and dangerous, particularly for us as hostages; in which case they might simply stand back and keep us under close surveillance.

On the other hand, they might not have sighted us at all, in which case they would be keeping a large area of these mountains under observation in the hope that they might happen to spot us.

For the time being, there was no way of knowing which of these possibilities was being explored by those seeking to rescue us.

But what of our captors? What would be their response to such a substantial military presence in the area?

In five or six hours, they could try, as they had successfully done before, to move us all out under cover of darkness. However, they would be aware that by then the military could have thrown that cordon right around the mountain and somehow they would have to break through it. The possibility that a close-quarters situation of this sort might lead them into an ambush would no doubt have been considered by the General and his commanding officers. They would know that a group of highly-trained military marksmen (especially if equipped with infra-red telescopic sights and laser-targeting weapons) could pick off many, if not all, of the guerrillas in our column, before they could use us as shields or shoot us. It would certainly be risky—for everyone involved, particularly us; but depending on how confident they were, they might just move in and try it as we moved out tonight.

As my thoughts careered on in this direction, another possibility suggested itself to my tired mind.

Ibrahim might send a couple of his men down the mountain with white flags to parley with his enemy.

His proposition might take one of many possible forms. For example, it might be a written ultimatum stating, perhaps, that we hostages were all alive and well, but that if any attempt was made by the Turkish military to move in on his guerrilla group, we would all be shot.

I began to fall into an exhausted sleep. These frightening imaginings became the first part of a nightmare.

An hour or so later, I awoke.

A number of the guerrillas were talking quietly on the ledge above. I could sense the tension as I sat up.

'What's happening now, Ron?' I asked.

Ron replied without turning his head. 'They're deciding whether or not they're going to shoot us.'

NOTES

1. The gospels were of course written by four men, each of whom was either an eye-witness to the events he recorded or was using eye-witness information from others. (See Lawrence O. Richards (ed), *The Applied Bible Dictionary*, Kingsway: Eastbourne, 1990, 'Gospels', p 445.) Within each Gospel there is an enormous amount of information concerning people, events, places and customs, all of which strongly indicate that the writers were recording carefully observed occurrences.

2. The Old Testament as a repository of highly specific information has long provided a rich and often verifiable resource for historians and archaeological researchers. 'Again and again, details such as titles given officials, descriptions of court practices, the terminology used in poetry, in cognate languages, and other minutae have refuted the critics and demonstrated the trustworthiness of the Bible' (Ibid, 'Archaeology' p. 87).

3. P.J. Wiseman, *New Discoveries in Babylonia About Genesis* (Marshall Morgan and Scott: London, nd).

4. Ibid, Chapters V, VII and VIII.

5. 'Hebrew and Chaldee Dictionary' in: *Strong's Analytical Exhaustive Concordance of the Bible* (nd), 'generations', 8435: The Hebrew word in the plural which is used, has in addition to the meaning *descent* (in the genealogical sense), that of *history*.

6. Genesis 6:10.

7. Ibid, 10:1.

8. The Biblical references indicating the names of these 'writers' are cited by P.J. Wiseman, op cit, as follows: Gen 5:1, 6:9, 10:1, 11:10, 11:27, 25:12, 25:19, 36:1, 36:9, and 37:2.

9. This flood account in Genesis gives, in addition to *what* and *where* checklist information, a great deal of *how*, *when* and *why* information which can have both direct and indirect relevance archaeologically. For example, the reference 'All the fountains of the great deep [were] broken up and the windows of heaven were opened' (Gen 7:11) tells something of the causes of the flood and also the conditions the ark would have to have withstood and survived.

10. In addition to general references such as that in *Encyclopedia Americana* (1986), 'Anchor' p 801, which describes 'the pierced stones used as anchors in ancient Egyptian records', and Thor Heyerdahl's article 'Tigris Sails Into the Past' (*National Geographic*, Vol. 154, no 6, Dec 1978, with photographs showing Heyerdahl holding a pierced anchor stone, p. 818) there are several detailed studies (see Chapter 2, note 81).

11. Suggestions that these stones might be part of a cemetery wall are quite without foundation. Whether standing upright or lying horizontally the stones are randomly situated; certainly not aligned in a way that might indicate a wall of some kind. Another suggestion that one of the stones photographed by the author appeared to have Turkish writing on it (which would presumably indicate its comparative modernity) is also without foundation. The photograph which very probably prompted this observation is reproduced in this book for the reader's own assessment on page 48.

12. When the author examined both these stones, they were lying horizontally just a few feet behind the Arzap stones that were standing vertically. About two-thirds of one stone were exposed above the ground. Both its underside and the other opening of its rope hole were still embedded in the hard clay and therefore could not be examined. Only a few square feet of the other stone which was close by were exposed. It was possible to examine the rope-hole of this stone, but only from the top. The author holds photographs of these stones on file. Drogue stones are functional objects although they can be decorated as a means of memoralising them. These two, however, appear to be quite bare. Since they were most likely buried for a long period, the people who erected and decorated the others standing nearby were probably not even aware of their existence—hence their pristine state.

13. This stone has drogue stone characteristics similar to those at Arzap. The shape, the size, the hollowed-out hole near the top are all virtually the same. This stone is also decorated. On the author's files are photographs of it and of its decorations. It is most unlikely that this very heavy artefact was transported to its present location. There seems to be no reason to suppose it was ever a tombstone or a marker. In 1990, the author located and photographed numerous ancient rock carvings in the mountain ranges of this area. These carvings are very similar to the ones on the Arzap stones which feature ancient crosses along with pagan symbols such as the Egyptian ankh. It is by no means impossible that all these carvings which feature crosses might be very ancient indeed—even pre-Christian, rather than post-Christian Arme-

nian. The cross symbol, like the ankh, was widely used long before Christ and was in fact a pagan symbol employed in Babylonian mysteries. It was actually a form of the mystic 'Tau' of the Chaldeans. (See A. Hislop, *The Two Babylons*, S.W. Partridge: London, 1871, pp 197-199, which incorporates information and diagrams. Also see L.A. Waddel, *The Phoenician Origin of Britons, Scots and Anglo-Saxons*, The Christian Book Club of America, Hawthorne, California 90250, 1983. Professor Waddel's work contains highly documented and extensively illustrated research data on the use of the cross symbol in the ancient Middle East and also in pre-Christian Europe.

14. Dr A. Snelling, *Creation ex nihilo*, Vol 14, No 4, September-November, 1992, p 34, col 2.

15. The hole in each case has been hollowed out so that a rope some inches thick can be drawn into it. The two openings of the holes are different sizes, in one instance measuring about eight inches in diameter at the front and only half that diameter at the rear. This design thus enables the knot of the rope to be drawn from behind the stone into the hollowed receptacle designed for it. The smaller opening at the back of the stone is not large enough to enable the knot to pull through. Once the stone is immersed in water, the knot swells becoming snug and tight within its circular cavern.

16. Most drogue stones discovered so far are much smaller than these, being only about 3 ft tall at the most. The possibility that the Arzap stones are drogue stones which might have been associated with the large boat-shaped formation has been postulated and explored by various researchers including ship's salvor David Fasold (see *The Ark of Noah*, Wynwood Press: New York, NY, 1988), William Shea, MD, PhD (See *CRS Quarterly*, pp 90-95, 'Origins', 82, 1981) and Ron Wyatt (see *Discovered: Noah's Ark!*).

17. Efforts by the author in 1992 to confirm seismologically the occurrence of an earthquake in the region around mid-1948 have not been successful. No event/earthquake above a magnitude of 5.5 to 6.0 has been located within the relevant area and time window. Unfortunately, due to the sensitivity of the seismic networks of those days, it is not possible to say what happened below the magnitude threshold cited above. (Correspondence Dr V.I. Marza, Romanian seismologist, to Dr A.S. Roberts, 18 January 1993.) It should be noted however that the sighting reported in the French press in 1949 rules out the possibility that the earthquake which revealed the formation occurred later than that year.

18. David Fasold, *The Ark of Noah*, pp 319-325.

19. Questions were tape-recorded in Kurdish. Each of these was answered in Kurdish and later translated by Necati Ates, a Kurdish mountain guide who had lived in the area. The tapes are held on the author's file. An unedited video tape of these late August, 1991 interviews along with details of where

and when they were made is held by Mrs M.N. Wyatt in Nashville, Tennessee, USA.

20. David Fasold, *The Ark of Noah*, pp 319-325. Although each of the three men interviewed by this author (Roberts) was asked to give a date for the earthquake which first brought the formation to light, none of them did. Even Reshit Sarihan, who earlier indicated a date in mid-May 1948, did not volunteer this specific information on the occasion of the interview organised by the author.

One particularly interesting comment was made by Hasan Ozer. He said, without any prompting, that 'we [the people of the nearby village] used to see *the light on the hill*, but there was no more light after the people who investigated the formation and ultimately identified it, had come.' The author, while perusing *The Travels of Marco Polo* came upon a footnote reference by Ibn Haukal to *Joudi*—the mountain on whose summit the ark rested. This was followed by Rennel's comment that *Jeudi* (this same mountain) 'is the part of the Carduchian mountains opposite to the Jezirat ibn Omar, *and that the dervishes keep a light burning there, in honour of Noah and his ark.*'

Could the light on the hill described by Hasan Ozer have been this light on Al Judi, which the dervishes have kept burning there down through the centuries 'in honour of Noah and his ark'?

21. *The Works of Flavius Josephus*, trs William Whiston (Ward Lock and Company: London, nd) I.iii.6.

22. Ibid.

23. Ibid.

24. Including Ron Wyatt, as stated to the author, John Baumgardner, *A Search for the Elusive Ark*, official newsletter, Los Alamos, August 19, 1988 and David Fasold *The Ark of Noah*, p 122.

25. The relatively recent emergence of the formation (around 1948) as described by our three eye-witnesses presents a substantial challenge to the notion that its shape is essentially the product of long-term valley-floor surface erosion. Although it is true that its shape assumed greater relief and clarity as a result of later tremors and stream erosion, its ship-like outline was apparent shortly after it became visible. Only about a decade after its appearance, this was clearly evidenced in early photographs taken from both the air and at ground level and from Reshit Sarihan's early comment, 'I know a boat when I see one' (D. Fasold, *The Discovery of Noah's Ark*, Sidgwick & Jackson: London, 1990, p 84). The available evidence suggests that the formation emerged as a boat shape. And this being so it would seem logical to assume that it was also boat-shaped for the period of its burial and perhaps even prior to that. Whilst it must be admitted that it is possible for boat-shaped natural formations to be buried then later revealed, it must also be admitted that it is possible for the same thing to happen to actual boats.

CHAPTER

6

Flag On The Mountain

The discussion among the guerrillas continued on the ledge above us.

We sat silent and still like absent plaintiffs being tried in some high court; awaiting a verdict which could shortly be handed down and summarily carried out at any moment.

As I looked around our small group I could see that some, if not most of them, were already appealing to a higher court—through prayer.

I had no idea what Ron had seen or heard to indicate that our lives might at this very moment be hanging in the balance. Perhaps, in spite of the language barrier, he had picked it up from their conversation, as one occasionally can do from a gesture or a word. Perhaps he had witnessed something down in the valley that I had missed when asleep; a verbal exchange or even a meeting between some of the guerrillas and the Turkish military that had given rise to a threat to execute us.

A hostage situation like ours can turn ugly very quickly. If such a situation becomes one of naked survival for a terrorist group, hostages can suddenly become that group's only means of getting out alive. In such a predicament, a technique commonly used is to announce that if they are not all guaranteed safe passage out of the area, they will start shooting their prisoners at regular intervals; and then if there is no such guarantee, to actually begin to do it.

Rather than discuss the basis of Ron's statement or indulge in conjecture about the present situation and its possible outcomes, I quietly prayed. I simply asked that God in his great wisdom and power might see fit to preserve us all in order that we might subsequently be useful to him and to others.

Down the mountain I heard the sound of branches being broken and undergrowth being trampled underfoot and pushed aside. After bird-whistle calls had been sent and received, the guards who had been deployed around the mountain returned. There was more talk between them and the other guerrillas, then they all began to pack up in preparation to leave.

Ibrahim came down to where we were sitting. A number of others with guns in hand and equipment on their backs came down as well.

What decisions had they made and what were they planning to do—in particular, with us?

Ibrahim crouched on his haunches. Cigarette in hand, he told us that we were all leaving.

It seemed that no one was about to be shot—at least not by them, if they were to be believed. The risk of our being shot in a confrontation with the Turkish military was quite another matter of course. When we asked about this risk, Ibrahim simply replied that the Turkish military constituted no problem.

My confidence failed to match his as the column formed up and we moved out from our little bower into the late afternoon sunlight.

Although we were all chest-deep in undergrowth, I was sure that we could have been easily observed from the ridge as we moved down and around to the back side of the mountain. When we reached the bottom of the slope there, we were made to wait while those on reconnaissance went ahead.

While we stood there, Ibrahim reiterated what he had said earlier about the military not being a problem. He told us also that he had recently heard a radio report that the military had been unable to locate us. To explain the term that had been used in the bulletin, he reached down and plucked up some pieces of dry grass. He held them in one hand, pointed to them, then mimed the action of sewing. He was playing charades with us again. Only after he had repeated these actions a couple of times did we realise what he was trying to tell us: that the search for us, as reported on the radio, was like looking for a needle in a haystack.

For the next three hours we trekked up through the forested foothills. Then we began to climb the high mountain we had seen earlier from our camp-site. The ascent was demanding and slow. Half-way up we stopped to drink from a swiftly flowing stream. Its waters were invigorating and cool; aerated upstream in the tumble, splash and swirl of a thousand tiny cascades.

The summit, when we attained it, stretched out before us like some immense airport tarmac, its length diminished only by perspective, its vanishing-point lost in the dusky distance of the night.

One of the guards took my arm. I was not quite sure why. Although the rocks and creeks had been occasionally difficult to negotiate, I had felt that I was managing reasonably well and did not need any assistance. By the time another half-hour had elapsed I was glad of his help. It had now become almost imposs-ible to avoid walking on the rocks and boulders that covered the ground everywhere in sharp angular profusion.

I am no stranger to stony terrain and have hiked over some very rough country in the Australian outback. But I had never experienced anything like this before. Half an hour of walking on these uneven and pointed rock surfaces began to take its toll on the soles of my feet. They began to bruise and then blister. In addition to this, there was the constant danger that a foot might slip down off one of those angled stones causing serious injury in the fall.

My guard, aware of my almost frictionless 'glass-bottomed' boots, sensed my trepidation. He held me firmly by the upper arm as one does a novice skater venturing falteringly onto the ice-rink.

How pleased we were when the column finally halted and we were able to take the weight off our chafed, aching feet! We had reached an interesting vantage point. We were on the edge of a precipice, from which could be seen the lights of another village down in the valley. Near the spot where we had stopped was a trig station, its tall steel pole and circular plate supported by a tripod that had been concreted to a rock platform. This was the highest point on the mountain.

Just as we were about to move on, two young guerrillas

unfurled a Kurdish flag. Then one of them shinned up the trig-pole. Gripping it tight with knees, feet and one hand, he reached down with his free hand, took the flag from his companion and attached it to the pole. As we set off again, I noticed the flag hanging there close to the pole, limp and motionless, like a coat in a cupboard; undisturbed by the cold mountain air.

As we moved out across these terrible rocks again, the idea that we might be left in some 'dormitory village' had almost faded from my mind. They were resolved, it seemed, to traverse this rock-cluttered plateau from one end to the other.

Within the next hour, the terrain became even more difficult. Everyone was having great trouble remaining upright. A number of the group, including at least one of our guards, fell very heavily. Ironically this guard, dazed by his fall, was helped to his feet by one of us, who fortunately stifled the involuntary response to pick up his gun for him.

As I looked ahead, I could just discern the other end of the mountain. It was about half a mile away.

Several hours of this tedious trekking had been putting heavy strain upon our muscles—not only on feet and legs, but on the upper trunk as we bent forward and back to keep our balance. At this rate we would not be off this rock-covered summit and down the mountain for at least an hour. I seriously doubted whether I would be able to manage it, unless they gave us an opportunity to rest up again. I guessed that the others weren't feeling much better than I was, so I just gritted my teeth and pressed on.

Suddenly and without warning my left foot, to which I had just transferred my weight, slipped right out from under me. I was momentarily air-borne, and knew at once that I would fall heavily. The left side of my head slammed hard against a large rock. I lay there unconscious for several seconds. As I lifted my head I tried to move my jaw. It was painful, but did not seem to be broken. I had fallen about six feet. The main force of my fall had been distributed evenly through the entire area of that side of my face. Furthermore, the angle of my head on impact must have matched exactly the angle of that part of the rock.

My guard climbed down and lifted me to my feet. I stood there unsteadily for a few moments checking my numb face and head for cuts, and continued to work my stiffening jaw. I seemed to have survived without injury. I looked down at the rock. It

bulged with sharp temple-shattering protuberances. I was
amazed that it was not covered at this moment with rapidly
congealing rivulets of my own blood and gratefully thanked God
that it wasn't.

It was almost 1 am when we reached the other end of the
mountain. I looked down to the wide barren valley floor, one and
a half thousand feet below. As I tried to focus on the mountains
across the other side, I suddenly realised I was not wearing my
long-distance spectacles. I checked my pockets, but they were not
there. I remembered having them on just after the raising of the
flag so they must have been jarred off when I fell. They are
probably lying there still awaiting the spade of some enthusiastic
young archaeologist, who, a thousand years hence, will perhaps
write a PhD thesis entitled *Myopia Among The Kurdish Rural Popula-
tion In the Late Twentieth Century*.

I recoiled at the thought that the guerrillas would take us
straight down this steep escarpment without even pausing to rest;
but that is precisely what they did. The young man who had been
helping me went on ahead. He was replaced by the soft-voiced
gentleman who had conferred with Ibrahim and was so expert at
butchering wild goats. He held my arm in a tight grip and began
to lead me down the gravel-covered clay surface of a slope that
had been deeply eroded by centuries of gushing water from desert
storms and melting snow.

Like the slope we had descended on the previous night, this too
was in dark moonless shadow. It was difficult and dangerous to
negotiate. Everyone in the column repeatedly lost his footing.
Some fell. However, my quiet-voiced helper did not allow me to
fall even once, but kept me upright and steady the whole way
down. Curiously enough, I was able to keep him from falling
heavily on two occasions when he lost his balance.

About halfway down, the column was allowed to stop and rest.
Thirsty and weary, I sat down, chin on my chest, arms extended
over my bent knees and hands dangling weakly over my shins.
After a minute or so, I lifted my head and looked up towards the
brow of the mountain, darkly brooding against the moonlit
clouds. My eye ran downwards over the long spur on which we
sat. We would be on the wide valley floor in less than half an
hour.

I wondered if there was any water down there.

'*Su, nerede?*' I asked my guard. He pointed towards the foot of the mountain.

It looked as dry as a bone to me. I thought I might have misunderstood his response, so I asked again. He pointed to the same area.

I was totally unconvinced—and totally wrong.

When we eventually reached the place, there it was; a well of wonderfully cool water, bountifully supplied by a spring which came, ironically, from that inhospitable mountain. I remembered, in an appropriately modified form, some verse written by the Australian poet C.J. Dennis:

> A great mother mountain
> And kindly is she
> Who nurses young rivers
> And sends them to me.

An hour later we were high up in the next mountain range and gasping for breath again. Except for three brief stops, we had been on the move for nine gruelling hours. The moment the column halted, my legs crumpled beneath me and I was almost instantly asleep, oblivious to the fact that the ground temperature was near freezing.

In twenty minutes, we were all up and on our way again, the column leader taking us on to a long spur that led to a tree covered ridge where I hoped we would camp. Suddenly, after only a few minutes climbing, I found that I was almost overwhelmed by an all-pervading weakness. It was not just in my legs, but in my mind; and, I feared, also in my will. I tried as best I could to keep going, but after barely a minute, had to stop.

I was stuck there in mid-stride, my forward leg on the slope; ready to buckle if I dared lift my other leg. I put both my hands on my knee to brace myself. And there I stayed, unable to take another step, as though welded to the mountainside.

The men in the column ahead of me climbed on, unaware that I had 'seized up'. The rest of the column were still quite a distance behind me, strung out in a long line down the slope.

I was aware from my studies in psychology that my urge to climb this mountain had suddenly been overcome— 'extinguished' is the technical term, I believe—by the more powerful urge not to climb it. This, I recalled, was not simply a matter of physical fatigue but rather a psychological mechanism. It had often been demonstrated experimentally with rats. They were first taught to run a maze and were rewarded with cheese each time they did it. However, when the cheese reward was repeatedly withheld, they became psychologically incapable of running the maze. In the jargon of the behaviourist psychologist, 'The continued withholding of positive re-inforcement [the cheese] had ultimately extinguished the learned response [running the maze].' Of course an ordinary Aussie layman would put it a bit more simply. He'd probably say, 'The rats, when they found out there was nothing in it for them, got browned off and went on strike.'

We five hostages for the last few days had been running the PKK maze. Like those laboratory rats, we had obediently performed all the activities set for us, trekking through mountains and valleys by night and hiding by day—all in the hope that we would be rewarded by being released. Yet each time an opportunity for our release had arisen, it had been ignored and we were made to push on—unrewarded. The conditions for producing psychological extinction were perfect. Little wonder I would not/ could not take another step! Of course I was willing to acknowledge that we were all hungry, thirsty and desperately tired, and this alone was almost enough to stop us in our tracks. However, the most satisfactory explanation for my present immobilisation was, I thought, this interesting psychological phenomenon. It certainly had nothing to do with the fact that I was fifty-nine years of age and was getting far too old for this kind of thing.

I was still summoning my resolve to continue climbing when a verse from The New Testament slipped quietly into my mind: 'In everything give thanks, for this is the will of God in Christ Jesus concerning you.'

The apostle Paul's term 'everything' seemed to cover this 'thing' which had happened to me. But could I give thanks in this helpless situation? I remembered having shared this very verse, before I left Australia, with my elder son's wife Julie, the day she was diagnosed as having advanced cancer. Julie was only thirty-one years old and had three young children ranging in age from seven to eleven.

In the turmoil of the initial shock and trauma of it all, I asked my daughter-in-law whether she was willing to give thanks to God. She said she was. She bowed her head right then and there and thanked him, not as the author of evil and sickness, but as the loving sustainer and strength of those who will thank and trust him in the midst of these things. Her life from that time until she died a little over a year later was a powerful testimony to the reality that God gives grace and strength to those who thank him in adversity—no matter how hopeless it may seem.

'If it was good enough for Julie,' I thought to myself, 'then it's good enough for me.'

I gave thanks to God, and somehow, took that next impossible step.

I thanked him again, then took the next one.

I cannot explain the psychological and physical mechanisms which operated as I continued for another half-mile up that slope to the mountain top. But I know that whatever it was, it was released and powered by some spiritual dynamic that began when I gave thanks to God as 'his will in Christ Jesus concerning me'.

When we reached the ridge at the top of the mountain, we found that half of the group had gone on ahead for some reason. The remaining half, including the five of us, was led by a tall, dull-eyed young man who, for the time he was in charge, did not exactly endear himself to us. Marvin and I were near the head of the column just behind him. Marvin had poor short-sight and I had poor long-sight. Unfortunately neither of us had good middle-distance vision, and seeing the rough ground on which we had to walk without our spectacles was quite a problem for us. Whenever we proceeded slowly to ensure that we did not slip or stumble, this man would berate us and impatiently beckon us on with *'Wheken! wheken!'* I had a suspicion that because of his particular quality of mind, any attempt by Marvin or myself to explain the subtleties of our eyesight problems would have been lost on him—even if we'd communicated it in fluent Kurdish.

So we said nothing. We just continued slowly and laboriously over the fragmented rocks and creek beds. Every now and then he would stop and try to urge us on. It made no difference to us of course, so he gradually settled into a sullen plod, like some dull draught-horse dragging a wagon with the brake on.

To make matters worse for the poor fellow, nobody answered

his cricket-chirp signals, with the result that we were soon completely lost. He then led us down the side of a deep ravine where we wandered aimlessly about, entertained only by his Kurdish cricket impersonations.

After a while he made us scramble up to the top of the ravine again. Eventually, more by accident than design, we came upon the other half of the group. They were already well settled, though uncomfortably, on a stony incline under the sparse foliage of a clump of spindly trees. It was here that we spent the few remaining hours of the night.

Next day we tried as best we could to catch up on a great deal of lost sleep. After lunch, we decided it was again time to talk to General Ibrahim about our release. Once more he was evasive. We tried to explain that our families did not know whether we were safe or not, or whether we were even alive. Ron pointed out that Richard was particularly concerned about his wife and family since he had two young children, one of them a severely handicapped little boy.

At this point, Ibrahim opened up an interesting avenue of discussion. He talked about allowing one of us permission to go to a nearby township or even to the city of Erzurum where he could tell the authorities that the rest of us were safe and well. Ibrahim added that if such a person, probably Richard, were so released, he would need to be blindfolded and then taken either on foot or perhaps on a donkey to some pick-up point from which he would travel the rest of the journey by bus.

Was his plan prompted by genuine concern for our families, especially for Richard's little boy? Or was it politically motivated; an attempt to show the world that we were not dead but being responsibly held in PKK custody? Perhaps the whole thing was nothing more than a means of buoying up the hopes of five hapless hostages—a whiff of cheese to keep the rats running their maze.

Whatever the plan or its genuineness, it was clear that Ibrahim had some further use for us in mind.

We stayed at this site for another night. Although it was not a pleasant place to bivouac, it did give us opportunity to recuperate from the fatigue accumulated over the previous two days. We waited expectantly for one of our number—hopefully Richard—

to be led out and released. However, nothing more was said of the proposal and nothing more was done.

Late in the afternoon of that day, our fifth as hostages, we broke camp and began to penetrate even further into the wild mountains.

Our journey that afternoon was only one of a number which was completed on several subsequent nights. On this particular occasion we trekked for miles along a dry valley which had the appearance of a recently blasted quarry, its jagged rocks having been fractured by the expansion and contraction of extreme mountain temperatures. On another occasion our journey took us down into the undergrowth of a densely forested gorge where we camped then slept with the sound of a rushing mountain stream in our ears. That particular journey, in spite of its scenic destination, was a most unpleasant one for Gary. During his descent he fell and damaged a ligament in his leg. The following night was even more unpleasant for him, since along with the rest of us, he was made to climb straight up the side of a valley which must have been at least five hundred feet high and sloped at an angle of almost sixty degrees. The surface of the incline was a treacherous mixture of loose stony gravel, slippery grass and beetling rocky outcrops. A number of the outcraps were actually ridges with cliffs which could not be skirted and had to be scaled in mountaineer fashion.

The climb was a dangerous and agonising ordeal for Gary. Yet he tackled it without complaint. As I watched him start his climb, I wondered how I would fare on those cliffs with my slippery-soled boots. Trying to find a secure foothold while wearing them would be difficult, I thought, but I could take them off and climb barefoot if necessary. I wasn't so confident about the slippery grass on that slope. However, as soon as I began my ascent, I found that I had at my disposal an array of 'nature's climbing ropes'. They were provided, courtesy of the mountain, in the form of slender saplings, their long flexible stems lying downhill and parallel to the slope. I found as I climbed that there was always one of them somewhere within reach, and that no amount of swinging or hand-over-hand tugging on my part could dislodge it.

We camped on the top of that mountain slope for two days. Even on the morning of our second day, there was not a sign of

Turkish forces anywhere. No planes, no helicopters and no troops. Our group appeared to have eluded the pursuers, if only for the time being. But although the military did not seem to be anywhere in our immediate vicinity, I was sure this was not an indication that the search had been called off. Extensive investigations would probably be under way in villages and farms right now. Clues that might suggest our direction of travel would be under close examination.

Almost certainly the PKK flag on that long stony mountain top would have been spotted and checked out by now. Would the Turkish military have assumed that it had been flown by our group? Quite possibly not. The PKK was very active throughout this south-eastern mountain region.

Was the Turkish army now aware of our present location? There was no way of knowing. However, we did know that the ridge where we had first sighted all those soldiers was only a two- or three-day march from here. Therefore it was quite likely that our rescuers might not be far behind us and could soon be using their air and ground reconnaissance to search this area where we were now hiding.

Our current location was high and tree-covered—an excellent place for someone who wanted to play a watching and waiting game; and this, I suspected, was precisely what General Ibrahim was doing.

There was little we five could do but watch and wait with him. While we did so, we sometimes talked—usually in a casual manner, one to one, rather than in a group, which, as Ron pointed out, might arouse suspicion in our guards.

In the course of one of our chats, Ron and I agreed that it would be impossible to get the dig done that summer. We discussed the need to re-apply for permission to do it the following year. Military protection would probably be a necessary condition for the granting of such permission.

Ron was no stranger to military protection. During 1985 he had gone to the Akyayla site with a radar research team that included Colonel James Irwin, the moon-walking astronaut. The Turkish authorities on this occasion had generously provided some thirty commandos to protect them. These men hid in the countryside surrounding the formation while the radar research proceeded. Iranian terrorists suddenly opened fire and although the researchers escaped unscathed, five terrorists and three Turkish soldiers lost their lives in the ensuing battle.

'Would the Turkish authorities be prepared to provide such military protection again?' I wondered. Whether they would be willing to run such risks to see the project brought to its conclusion was difficult to answer. I was sure however that we in the team were still highly motivated to finish the job, even though we might be personally at risk in doing so.

We all sensed an urgency about it because of the marked deterioration evidenced at the site. The sides of the formation which were so well-defined only a few years ago were now in a number of places jagged and fragmented. Snow-melt and stream erosion had removed much of the mud from around the formation and were now undermining it. This, together with the weight of the overburden inside the formation, was causing the walls to collapse outwards. When the external walls of a house begin to collapse, it is not long before its inner structures—floors and ceilings—start to collapse as well. Ron had already noted that several mud areas under the 'deck' of the formation that were previously high were now low or sunken, suggesting that the process of internal collapse was already underway.

Were there still open areas inside—chambers or cabins perhaps with decks, walls and doors intact? If there were, we wanted to get inside and examine them before they were squashed flat and the formation reduced to little more than a heap of rubble.

My mind went back to our discussions with the Turkish authorities a little over a week earlier. On that occasion we had expressed our concern about this deterioration and how a dig might be carried out without accelerating it. Methods of short- and long-term protection of the formation had been discussed, along with plans to house it under some kind of permanent covering.

As I relaxed there in the shade, I began to imagine what might follow if a preliminary dig should bring forth the kind of evidence that would establish and confirm beyond any doubt that this object was indeed the ark of Noah. Should that happen, I could see the site commanding unprecedented world-wide attention. It would also attract the kind of funding required to investigate, preserve and develop it properly. Its protective dome would house the world's oldest maritime museum where the public could observe its ongoing archaeological programme from year to year. The implications for a wide range of disciplines, particularly history, science and religion would be vast, I thought.

A preliminary dig was essential. But as things were right now, there was some doubt as to whether any of our team would be around next year to encourage or see it done.

There were times while we camped at this location when we were able not only to talk together about these things but also to think quietly and pray—particularly for our families, who in the absence of any specific information over these last few days, would be starting to fear the worst. How I longed to send a message to Margaret and the family, no matter how brief, just to let them know that we were still alive and reasonably well. For me, the most difficult part of the whole situation was realising that they knew nothing of our fate. I sensed the anguish they would feel and knew the frustration of being totally unable to alleviate it.

I was sure that because of this, our loved ones were having a far more difficult time than we were. So in the absence of phone calls, faxes or letters from me, I prayed that my family would be sustained and encouraged directly by God. I have long believed that prayer is beneficial—for both the pray-er and the pray-ee. And here was an instance, when in the complete absence of telephone communication prayer may well have produced some positive outcomes.

For almost a week now we had marched, eaten, slept and performed all the other basic functions which hostages must perform—without the benefit of water with which to wash ourselves. For those who live in Western society, cleanliness is next to godliness; but for us, it was next to impossible. Our grimy unwashed bodies and soiled clothes had given to each of us what might best be described as 'an air of social unacceptability'. There was really nothing any of us could do about it. So we all disregarded our mutual hygiene problems and interacted with one another just as normal sweet-smelling people with laundered socks and mint-fresh breath might do.

On this basis, Marvin and I sat chatting together. As we talked, he noticed that the heel of my left boot had been almost torn off. Marvin, ever helpful and resourceful, took a small penknife from his pocket—the kind that has an assortment of blades and implements that fold away neatly with a satisfying click but can be prized out again only at the risk of breaking a fingernail. Choosing the appropriate implement, a sharp-pointed little metallic skewer which we used to call a 'pig-stabber' when I was a boy, Marvin asked me to remove my boot—the most unpleasant part of the exercise. Then, skilfully wielding his pig-stabber, he began to drill a number of holes in the heel and the upper. Reaching into another pocket, he found, to my amazement, a spare shoe-lace. He threaded it through those holes in such a way that by tying it above the instep, the boot was repaired.

What a clever fellow Marvin was! His cleverness had nothing to do with his skill as a high-flying American business consultant. Marvin the business consultant was totally irrelevant out here on the hostage trail. But Marvin the bootmender—now here was a man of relevance! The person who was able to mend my boot was giving me back my mobility—maybe even ensuring my survival.

I thanked him. Then, finding myself a shady spot under the trees, I lay down for my morning nap. As I made myself comfortable, I began to wonder whether any of the vocations we five esteemed so highly in our Western culture would have relevance or value in the eyes of our Kurdish captors.

The fact that Richard was owner-manager of a travel agency and an expert tour director would be of no relevance to them or their current travel itinerary; in any case, the vacancy for their tour director job had already been filled.

Ron, a highly competent anaesthetist back in the United States, was a striking example of professional redundancy here in Eastern Turkey. Nobody in the entire group had the slightest trouble going to sleep. On the contrary, everybody's problem seemed to be that of staying awake. The last person we needed was a sleep doctor.

Then there was Gary, our London antiques salesman: a specialist in toy soldiers. What did these guerrillas care about toy soldiers, when they were absorbed in playing deadly war games with real ones?

And if anyone would be regarded as irrelevant it would have to be me. What possible interest could these Marxist revolutionaries have in my academic research of history when they were busy making it?

How radically a change of circumstances can challenge our view of what and who are really important in life.

I was beginning to drift off as these topics floated around inside my mind—anaesthesia, directing tours, shooting soldiers and mending boots. I had the feeling, as I dropped off to sleep, that Marvin's bootmending had the edge.... I was awakened around noon by what sounded like a woman's voice.

A woman on this remote mountain?

I heard it again. It belonged to a woman all right. Of that I was certain, even though I could not see her.

I sat up and there she was; standing just down from the area where we were all lying. A young woman, about thirty years of age, of short stature and dressed in a khaki army uniform. She seemed out of place here with us; not so much because she was a woman, but because of her clothing. Her tailored army jacket and trousers were spotless. They looked as if they had just been pressed. Her thick dark brown hair was brushed back from her forehead and temples. It was held in place—every strand of it— by two curved black combs. Her not unattractive face was smooth-complexioned and intelligent. Its shape was not that of the typical Kurdish woman. It was broader and rounder. As she turned to speak to one of our guards, I noticed that in profile, her facial features were somewhat flat, giving her a slightly oriental appearance.

Her manner was confident but feminine. As she came up to meet the five of us, we stood to be introduced. Interesting how the presence of a woman, even a guerrilla woman, can give a touch of decorum to a group of men.

With a functionally manicured left hand, she touched her chest and identified herself.

'Dilah,' she said, enunciating the name clearly, repeating it to ensure that we would get it right. Then, with almost parade-ground formality, she shook our hands as we introduced ourselves.

This having been done, Ron, with all the charm of the deep south, invited her to sit down. As she sat cross-legged in front of us, I wondered how she managed to stay so clean.

I felt embarrassed by our disreputable state.

'Well,' I said to myself, 'it's not our fault. It's because of people like you and Ibrahim that we all look and smell the way we do.'

'*Sprechen Sie Deutsch?*' she asked.

We all shook our heads. None of us spoke German.

'*Je parle Français un peu,*' I said, '*parlez-vous Français, Dilah?*'

She shook her head. She didn't speak French.

'*Espagnol?*' asked Marvin, who spoke Spanish fluently.

Dilah shook her head again. She didn't speak that either. 'We all speak English,' added Gary. 'English and some Turkish.'

She did not respond.

'Do you speak any English?' asked Gary.

'A little only,' she replied with a Germanic tilt of her head and shrug of her shoulders.

The billiard ball had bounced off every cushion, missed every pocket, and was now in an almost impossible position on the table.

I could see another agonizingly slow conversation coming up.

However, in the next half-hour or so, we managed with difficulty to engage in some reasonably meaningful exchanges.

Dilah, it seemed, was a German-born Kurd who had been educated in Bonn and had completed about two years of nursing there before joining a PKK military training programme in Germany.

She was obviously very committed to the cause and had no qualms about proudly stating all these things openly to us. She said that PKK guerrillas were trained in other countries too. She told us that the group which had taken us was only one of many operating throughout Eastern Turkey. She added that Ibrahim was the General co-ordinating several groups in this mountain region. Presumably, Dilah had come from one of these groups herself and it was probably stationed not far away.

We asked her whether she knew anything about plans for our release.

Like Ibrahim, she was evasive and simply inquired about how we were managing. We told her we were looking forward to being released and having a bath. She said there was a place nearby where we would soon be taken to have a bath.

The bath sounded fine, but a bath following our release sounded even better. So pressing her again on the question of our release, I assured her, as I had Ibrahim, that when they let us go we would be willing to affirm we had not been badly treated. I asked Gary to hand me the little dictionary with the Turkish statement on its fly-leaf to that effect.

He gave it to me and I passed it to Dilah. She read it, then tapping it with the back of her hand said,

'It is not enough.'

As she stood up to leave, we all began to wonder what would be 'enough'.

Would an arrangement to release us in exchange for several Kurdish political prisoners be enough?

Perhaps several years as prisoners chained up in some village cellar to be released only at the birth of a Turkish Kurdistan would be enough.

Or perhaps an ultimatum by the PKK to execute us one month from now unless certain PKK demands were met—would that be enough?

Prospects for our release were not good.

CHAPTER

7

Guerrilla Children

I t was Friday, 6 September 1991.
　　At 8 o'clock it would be exactly one week since we had been kidnapped.

We talked together over lunch about Dilah's conversation with us. What was the purpose of her visit? She was certainly not here by accident. From her comments and general demeanour, it was clear that she held a position of some rank.

My left leg had become swollen because of the continual heavy trekking. This was not unusual. An hour or so walking was generally enough to cause not only swelling but also pain and cramps in that leg. I had learned over the years to disregard these symptoms. It was giving me a good deal of trouble now though, so I stood up to exercise it for a bit.

As I stretched my legs and walked a few yards along the clearing, I noticed a pair of dainty feet protruding from under the bushes. They belonged to Dilah. She was sound asleep. It was siesta time for most of the group.

The afternoon heat, and time itself, hung heavily upon me. After being wrenched from one extreme of stressful and dangerous marching to the other of fitful over-exhausted sleep, I was finding it hard to wind down. Physically, I was probably going through a period of withdrawal from an adrenalin high. Psychologically, I was struggling to come to terms with the possibility that none of us would be going anywhere—perhaps for a long time.

I went back and sat down next to my drowsy friends. I began to think about the project and our total inability to get back to it now. I imagined the formation just sitting there, begging to be excavated, and felt the frustration of not being able to get to it.

I hoped that the oncoming winter and the erosion of the thaw would not wreak too much havoc before next summer. There was nothing we could do about it right now, and worrying was foolish. So I tried to content myself with the thought that our recent visit to the site had resulted in some positive outcomes.

I began to think about the petrified antler-tip that was embedded in the mud-cast of the western wall when I found it. I suspected that it might have been laid bare as a result of erosion or perhaps by an extrusion process caused by outward pressure from within the formation. There seemed to be no reason why this and the other antler fragment that had been found on site could not be very specifically identified and placed geographically.

Similarly the animal dung, although now fossilised, could be analysed and identified too. Such identification could tell us the kind of animal and the food it had been eating. I had been assured that there were people whose biological speciality was the study of petrified animal dung. Would they be able to identify specifically the animal or animals represented in our sampling of coprolites? What could they suggest about their diets? Would those diets suggest that the animals had been grazing somewhere in the area where the coprolites were found, or had they been hand-fed as would be necessary if they had been on board a ship for some time?

The animal hairs might also be very significant. The ones I had been able to examine personally had been taken from inside the formation. If our formation were indeed a boat, then pieces of hair from inside it could yield some very important information. Hair is capable of surviving for great periods of time—as in the case of hair of Egyptian mummies and corpses retrieved from the earth. There seemed no reason why hairs embedded in the mud inside the formation could not be submitted to detailed scientific analysis. I was sure that if this were done, the legal experts doing it could identify the samples in much the same way as they identify human and other hair samples for legal purposes.

When I had been in Britain a few months earlier I had made

inquiries about having such samples forensically analysed and had discussed it with Ron. We agreed that the considerable expense that would be involved would nonetheless be justified— especially if a careful dig were to bring forth evidence of hair from a wide range of animal types which were not indigenous (and never had been) to this area of Turkey.

Costs were a constant problem. Laboratory analyses are very expensive, especially when there are so many samples involved. I hoped that the people to whom Ron and I had spoken about financial assistance would soon see their way clear to assist in this way, especially in this important area of scientific analysis.

Perhaps the most interesting find to come out of our recent trip to the site was the object that looked like a rivet or bolt head surrounded by a washer. Whether this object had been liberated by erosion from the 'hull' wall, or had simply been thrown or dropped there by local children, was difficult to say. However, the specimen was a most unusual and important one.

The 'head' appeared to have hammer marks on it. Those who had been aware of the presence of metals on the site were already wondering whether this was an example of one of the suspected metal 'joining mechanisms' detected within much of the formation.

Students of the Genesis account had pointed out that it contains an interesting reference to metallurgical sophistication, where Tubal-Cain is said to have worked in metals (Gen 4:22). I thought about the large number of hidden metal objects which seemed to be distributed throughout the formation in that regular pattern. How enlightening it would be if a dig should determine exactly what they were—examining them *in situ*, then analysing samples in laboratories. What would they turn out to be? More rivet-like objects, perhaps spikes or brackets? Hopefully it would be possible also to determine their function, as we related them to the structures in which they were embedded. And the structures themselves; how informative it would be to extend the information already gained about them from subsurface investigation, by laying them bare! If there were walls, decks, bulkheads and ribs within the formation, an excavation would enable them to be examined 'hands on' in detail. Depending on the state of their preservation, a great amount of information could be gained about them, not just as individual artefacts but as parts of a whole.

I could not help comparing what existed under the mud on the site with what lay under the earth-covering in England at Sutton Hoo, the site where an ancient Anglo-Saxon vessel had been buried for centuries beneath its mound. I had studied this site several years earlier and knew that when it was being excavated, archaeologists had found that there was virtually none of the hull left. However, the shape of the hull along with its ribs, and with other structures, was still able to be accurately plotted and reconstructed from nothing more than rusted blobs of metal—originally joining mechanisms. We had similar indications of metals on the Akyayla site—and much, much more.

A host of questions had already stirred many imaginations. Some of the people who had followed the research on this site in Turkey were now beginning to wonder whether an excavation might bring some archaeological answers to numerous ark questions:

- how and where so many animals could be fitted on board,
- how food and water were stored,
- the nature of the cabins for humans and cages for animals,
- the nature of the door by which the humans and animals would have entered, and
- what the window was that is mentioned in the Genesis account as being 'a cubit above'.

Was it possible that these and a multitude of other ark questions might soon have answers that were now only a dig away?

It was my own hope that there might still be some open spaces within the formation that had not yet collapsed and could still be entered. A tantalisingly fanciful thought crossed my mind; I could not help indulging it. 'If this turns out to be the ark and we manage to get inside the thing,' I thought to myself, 'maybe we'll be able to throw some light on the statement in Genesis 6:4 that 'there were giants in the earth in those days.' Like many others who had examined this interesting reference, I too had wondered, since it referred to the pre-Flood world, whether giantism (like longevity) was being indicated as the norm for that time. If so, then Noah and his family as pre-Diluvians might well have been giants also. In order to check this possibility I resolved with a quiet chuckle that one of the first things I would do if I did get inside was to check the size of the doors and bunks.

Would we find drogue stones inside the formation? I seemed to remember that Ron Wyatt had already suggested this as a distinct possibility. If they were there, then this would indicate a strong link between them and other stones tentatively identified as drogues in the region.

I felt myself drifting off to sleep in the heat...

Later in the afternoon we received a visit from a young lad no more than fifteen years of age. I assumed that he had accompanied Dilah on her journey here.

He was bright-eyed and pleasant; boyishly enthusiastic. He talked about his school-mates who were also involved with the PKK. He told us, too, that he had just received news that one of them had recently been killed.

What effect would this have upon this young man's intrinsically pleasant personality? Would he soon be locked into the revenge syndrome, to be soured and hardened by it for the rest of his precarious life?

As soon as our evening meal was over, it was time to move out. The immediate plan was to take us to a *yayla*—a sort of village retreat in the mountains, where we would have our much-needed bath.

Ibrahim was not with us when we left; the group was led by Dilah. For someone with such short legs, she set a brisk pace. Gary's painful ligament injury made it necessary for him to be assisted at the rear of the column. After several hours marching and several stops to check with reconnaissance, Dilah announced that we would not be able to go to the *yayla*. The Turkish military were there, she said, so our journey had to be re-planned accordingly. Tonight would not be our bath-night, it seemed.

Our new route took us through an area which was obviously considered dangerous. We were cautioned to walk quietly and quickly. As we hurried along the side of a wide bare valley, we repeatedly set farm dogs barking. In spite of this, there was no human challenge to our presence.

Ultimately, we found ourselves ascending a steep treeless ridge near the top of which was a forest of oak saplings. There we were met by two guerrillas who were not part of our group. With them was an elderly man who wore the rough clothes of a farmer—a coarse shirt buttoned up to the neck, thick coat and trousers, heavy boots and dark cap. His unshaven face was deeply lined and tanned. Perhaps he owned this land, or at least grazed his stock on it.

He greeted us warmly with the firm clasp of a work-worn hand. In his other hand he held a battered tin ladle. He handed it to Richard, then motioned him to a small ditch on the ridge in which a shallow puddle of spring water overflowed and trickled down the slope.

When it was my turn to use the ladle I found the water surprisingly clean and fresh to drink. After everyone had drunk his fill and washed his face and hands, I determined to seize the opportunity to wash some of my clothing.

So I quickly slipped my arms out of my boiler-suit and removed my sweat-stained T-shirt. Plunging it into the downstream part of the spring, I squeezed it and watched the bubbles rise. Then I lifted it to the surface and began to rub the underarm sections with the best soap substitute of which I was aware—the dark-brown silt of the stream.

To my surprise, the old man tapped me on my bare shoulder and handed me an oblong cake of soap—the rough abrasive kind my pioneer grandmother used to make in the pre-supermarket era.

It was time to move on, so I hurriedly wrung out my shirt, thanked the old gentleman and took my place in the column. How I would have loved to have wallowed like some gleeful hippopotamus in the oozy cleansing mud of that little spring, or even to have taken enough time to wash that article most needful of laundering—my underpants.

'Well,' I thought as we moved into the forest, 'perhaps bath night/laundry night is not too far away.'

I was expecting several more hours of trekking, but found to my delight that our next camp-site was right there—just within the forest.

It was already occupied by another guerrilla group. They greeted our band, including the five of us, in a warm friendly fashion. Most of them shook our hands and several identified themselves by name.

It was a large group—perhaps larger than ours. The two

groups together must have numbered close to thirty. A tall gaunt-faced young man of around nineteen or twenty years of age introduced himself to us in halting but quite intelligible basic English. His name was Çia. He was a university student who had recently left his studies to join the PKK. Two young girls also introduced themselves. One of them claimed to be only thirteen years of age; her friend was barely a year older. I could not help thinking that they were mere children—though dressed in their khaki uniforms and armed with guns and grenades, they were children nonetheless; the youngest only a little older than my eldest grandchild.

Guerrilla boys and girls

Most children of that age in the West would be still under their parents' care and supervision. There was simply no parallel in our society for what these youngsters were doing. This was certainly no youth training programme. Nor was it a safety-guaranteed cadet school, where the skills of war could be learned without hazard. This was the real thing—an in-service 'train as you live or die course' where the bullet that brings death knows nothing of youth or age.

As we continued along the clearing we were greeted by a little man whose pudgy face radiated an impish sense of fun. He had heavy black brows and eyes that twinkled as he spoke. He walked with a slightly humorous gait, his feet wide apart and his toes pointed outwards. He had about him just a touch of the camp clown, I thought. However, when I came close to him, the comic image faded and was replaced by that of the grim guerrilla.

Protruding from his lower left cheek was a bullet which had lodged in his jawbone. It was suppurating profusely. A number of others had also been wounded, but, like this good-humoured little fellow, seemed largely unperturbed by their injuries. We began to prepare ourselves for what promised to be a very cold night. The altitude of this campsite was higher, I suspected, than that of previous ones. The camp fire was now just a greying heap of dying embers. The guerrillas never added wood to keep their evening fires going, but let them die out and re-lit them next morning—probably a precaution to avoid being located.

As the night wore on, the small threadbare blankets which each of us had been handed proved to be woefully inadequate. They were too thin to provide much warmth and too small to cover the sleeper's whole body at the one time. Consequently most of my body was cold for most of the time and some for part of it—a leg, a shoulder, a foot—was always exposed and nearly freezing. The two hours before sunrise were the worst. None of us got much sleep then. How pleased we were, when dawn broke and the fire was blazing again.

Within an hour the entire camp was buzzing with activity. However, the constant movement of people was somehow different to what we had experienced before. To be sure, the cooks in this camp were busy as they had been at our previous campsites—perhaps rather more so because now there were more mouths to feed. Guards were changed and posted just as efficiently as before. Routines were similar also.

But there was something different about the atmosphere, which had to do with a change of function. The purpose of this camp was not simply to take care of five hostages. That was only part of it. This was essentially a military camp within which strike-force campaigns were being planned and from which sorties were being launched.

In the course of the morning, small fully-armed groups moved out. They were clearly going on manoeuvres.

Dilah constantly moved back and forth giving orders to both men and women. She appeared to be in charge, and handed down instructions concerning most of the activities which were going on. Her commands were promptly and quietly obeyed. In spite of this group's rag-tag attire and lack of military spit and polish, its discipline was high. No one questioned an order. No one complained or covertly commented when unpleasant tasks were given. Obedience was total, even in the youngest.

As for Ibrahim, we rarely saw him. He had his own little area down the slope off among the trees, away from the others. He rarely emerged from there; probably, I assumed, because he was formulating, planning and directing those operations which were his responsibility as a regional commanding officer.

Even with his knowledge of the local terrain and maps to aid him, his task would be difficult. As far as I could ascertain, he did not have the benefit of two-way radio and would therefore need to do all his group co-ordination on the ground using runners; a cumbersome and time-consuming business, but probably better than running the risk of having his radio signals picked up and pinpointed by the Turkish military.

Around 10 o'clock that morning, the highly militarised nature of our location became disturbingly apparent. Helicopters began to hover over the adjacent mountains. The throb of their engines and whirr of their rotors was accompanied by long bursts of gun-fire.

Perhaps those in the helicopters were shooting at some of the men who had earlier been right here with us and were now patrolling those mountains. Or perhaps the guerrillas were firing at *them*. Some of their weaponry was large enough to do considerable damage to a helicopter and might even bring one down. It was possible, too, that the helicopters were being used to set down troops, and this was covering fire for them.

Whatever was going on, it was fairly certain that we were now in the middle of a war zone and the guerrillas who were holding us were well and truly engaged in its hostilities.

I watched these young Kurds as they performed their camp duties. In this role they were unhurried and courteous—not unlike the majority of their countrymen, whose kindness and hospitality I had often sampled and enjoyed in Eastern Turkey. It was difficult to see them in their death-dealing guerrilla role.

Those gentle young hands of the girls who daily served us life-sustaining food and drink—could they be the same hands that loaded the guns and hurled the grenades to destroy life?

Those strong male arms that supported us as we stumbled and fell—surely they could not be the arms that powered the gun butts as they rammed and cracked the skulls of fallen Turkish troops?

And those soft Kurdish eyes—could they be the eyes that go cold and hard as they hold the enemy in steadying gunsights; and then, passionless, at the squeeze of a trigger, watch him spin and fall?

There were two faces, it seemed. Which was the real one?

The deep personal conflicts which would already have been generated in each of these young people could be only imagined. And how these conflicts could ever be effectively resolved or even rationalised was quite beyond me.

As hostages, we were having our own problems adjusting to the situation. Here we were, held captive by a band of guerrilla terrorists who were being hunted by thousands of Turkish troops. Wherever these guerrillas went, we went. Wherever they hid, we hid. We ate what they ate and slept where they slept. Like it or not, we were totally dependent on them. And because they had supplied all our basic physical needs, we had gradually—oh so gradually—come to think of them as benign benefactors rather than trained killers. The overtly military function of this camp had confronted me with an unpleasant fact which I had so far been unwilling to face; that these young people had not signed on to look after hostages like us. Their primary task was to harass and kill Turkish soldiers—who were the very people risking their lives to rescue us.

And here was I, subconsciously identifying with them. The very idea that I—one who had always sought to uphold the law and the sanctity of the individual—should do this was repugnant to me. I recoiled from it.

How does one come to terms with such a dilemma?

One does what most do. One rationalises.

That is exactly what I began to do. I began by attempting to justify myself, and my friends too.

'We didn't ask to be taken hostage. We had absolutely no say in the matter. And right now we are powerless to do anything. There's certainly nothing any one of us can possibly do to stop them from killing their enemies, even though these enemies are in reality our allies and friends.'

'The fact of the matter is,' I went on to tell myself, 'that we are totally under their control. If we are to survive, all we can do is obey their orders. The fact that they are killing our friends is beyond our control. We cannot be held responsible.'

Logical and practical as this rationalisation seemed at first, I gradually became aware that there was no real justification for me in it. As I ran it through in my mind, I realised, with a shudder, that this was precisely the kind of reasoning employed by German war criminals at Nuremberg to absolve themselves of responsibility. They too said,

'I am not responsible. There was nothing I could do to prevent these terrible things from happening. I was acting under orders.'

This was their plea. Would it be mine?

'Of course not,' I rationalised again. 'It is not the same for me. I did not actively collaborate with our captors in such things. I did not kill or even desire to kill anyone.'

To a point, this was of course true. But I knew that something else was also true. The German guards who were involved in the atrocities at Dachau and Belsen began with similar rationalisations to these. Like me, they had first chosen to ignore the unpleasant truth about those with whom they were associating. Like me, they had also gone for cover behind the chain-of-command argument. They were nonetheless collaborators. And their collaboration had begun in the mind. That was where each of them had first capitulated and identified with those who controlled them. From then on, the ensnared mind generated and tolerated thoughts which in turn fathered deeds—atrocious deeds, which to Germany's undying shame, still stand condemned by the world at large.

Had I already capitulated in my mind? Was I already identifying with these guerrillas and their behaviour?

I remembered Patty Hearst, daughter of an American newspaper magnate, who many years ago was kidnapped by a left-wing group and ended up wielding one of their guns and helping them rob a bank. Given enough time, stress and psychological coercion, could we too be pushed to such active collaboration?

I prayed we wouldn't.

Later that same morning two of our guards began to tell us, with undisguised enthusiasm, about their armed exploits. They claimed to have recently attacked a Turkish vehicle somewhere in this region. Because of language limitations, it was not possible for us to find out whether the occupants of the vehicle were injured or killed. They told us also how they had successfully ambushed a train. In addition to this information, we were told that a Turkish soldier had been recently killed in a mountain skirmish. I feared that if the information were correct, this man might well have been one of the troops out looking for us.

The general impression I gained from these reports was that in its war to separate Eastern Turkey the PKK was having some success. I suspected, though, that these snippets of propagandist information had been specially prepared for our ears.

In the afternoon a radio newsflash was picked up and communicated to the entire camp. Apparently, some PKK spokesman had just announced that anyone intending to travel in Eastern Turkey would henceforth be required to apply for a visa from the PKK. Perhaps our widely reported kidnapping had emboldened the PKK to make this announcement which, it seemed to me, was actually a warning to future travellers and at the same time a PKK claim to sovereignty over the region.

Dilah was delighted by this announcement and sought us out to share it. Early next day, she came over to us to share a further piece of information. This time, her mood was serious. She sat down with the air of one who has just received bad news.

'Turkish Military', she said, in a tremulous voice that barely disguised her anger, 'burn forest.'

She made a broad gesture to indicate that this was a widespread practice.

She stood up, looked into the distance, then as though talking to herself, added with a frown, 'This—very bad.'

She did not look down at us to gauge our reaction, but walked away without further comment.

For the PKK, this tactic certainly was bad. To burn the only forest cover they had in order to flush them out was serious indeed; not only for them but for us.

I looked across at Marvin. I knew that this news had brought to his mind, as well as mine, a conversation that we'd had in Ankara, just prior to our capture. We had gone to a bank to arrange for a credit-card advance. Having encountered some technical problems at the teller's window, the manager came out to help us. With typical Turkish hospitality, he apologised for the problem and invited us to come into his office where Marvin and I sat and chatted with him as we sipped some *çay*.

In the course of our conversation he shared his concerns about the Kurdish problem. He was not Kurdish, nor was he a terrorist or PKK sympathiser, he said. However, he told us of his fear that the mountains of Eastern Turkey might soon be denuded by forest fires, lit as a means of locating and destroying the PKK. He said that if this were to occur, there would be a terrible blood-bath throughout the Eastern provinces.

As I looked across at Marvin, I knew that he remembered all this too, and was probably asking similar questions to the ones now racing through my mind:

Did this fire-lighting ploy mark the beginning of this next phase?

Would it escalate into the kind of holocaust feared by that Turkish bank manager?

And had the search for us triggered it off?

Following the mid-morning news broadcast, Dilah told us that the search for us had been called off. She claimed that the newsreader had said that we 'seemed to have disappeared from off the face of the earth'. We were not sure, of course, that what Dilah told us was true. And surely, if the Turkish authorities had put such a massive troop force into the field, they would not have withdrawn it after only eleven or twelve days; especially in view of the fact that the Germans who had been taken hostage before us were released after only ten days. In spite of these doubts, the possibility that the search was now over was a sobering one for all of us. We knew that searches like this one were discontinued only when those organising them felt that the missing people were either dead or hidden where they could not possibly be found.

None of us discussed this matter at any length. However, we all knew that if it were true, the news would be very hard for our families to bear. Before lunch we prayed especially for them as well as for those others, including our captors, for whom we usually prayed each time we gave thanks for our food.

As soon as the midday meal was over, most of the men and women in the group sat down in the shade and began to write letters. When they had finished them, they folded them up and handed them to one of the young girls who was acting as postmistress.

Then Ibrahim emerged. He lit a cigarette and sat down with us to talk. He inquired about how we were getting along. We told him we were doing all right. What else could we say when members of his group continued to function without the slightest complaint despite being punctured by bullets?

He then asked us whether there was anything in particular that we would like. Our response (which we gave almost in chorus), that we would like to go home was politely ignored. He reiterated his offer, earnestly indicating that if any one of us really wanted something, he would arrange to get it.

It sounded suspiciously like a last request to me.

However, thrusting this fleeting thought from me, I decided to take his offer at face value. Ron asked for *karpuz* (watermelon); I asked for some notepaper and pens so that we could write letters home, as the guerrillas had done.

To my surprise, this request was granted almost at once. Within a few minutes, each of us had received a pen, a small piece of note-paper and instructions to complete our letters within ten minutes if we wanted to catch the mail. In my letter, I sought to assure Margaret that we were all reasonably well, that we had not been starved or mistreated and were hoping that we would soon be released. I assured her that I was praying for everyone at home and sent my love to her and the family.

Dilah took each letter as it was finished and perused it to ensure, I supposed, that we had not said anything derogatory about the PKK, or hidden cunningly-coded messages concerning our whereabouts.

Knowing how limited Dilah's English was, I doubted whether her censorship would amount to much. Perhaps she would get university-trained Çia to check out our letters using his superior English. She quickly glanced through my letter as I briefly explained what I had written, then folded it up and put it with the others. She assured us that all the letters would be taken across the mountains to Erzurum by three guerrillas (two men and a girl), who would mail them there.

'Erzurum,' I thought. 'That would be a huge journey from here—dangerous, too. Why would they go to Erzurum? Surely they would find it easier to head for Bingol which would be much closer, then leave the mail in some friendly village nearby, to be posted more safely by a local.'

While I didn't doubt that the letters penned by the guerrillas would be mailed, I was not so optimistic about ours. However, because we so much wanted those letters to go to our loved ones, we chose to believe—probably quite naively—that they would all be mailed, just as we'd been told they would. We began to calculate how long it might be before they would leave Turkey and be delivered to our families. We even set dates for their arrival.

I suspected that like me, the others also had their doubts. If they did, nobody voiced them. Just to have written those letters had been somehow therapeutic. And part of the therapy was believing they would be sent, received and read.

I could see Ibrahim down at the bottom of the clearing. He was talking to Dilah. What were they saying, I wondered?

Perhaps they were quietly congratulating themselves on having made a modest investment of five pieces of paper and the use of a few pens to make a nicely manageable profit—five hostages who would be reasonably happy for about a week.

Late that afternoon, just after our evening meal, the three young people designated to handle the mail began to say goodbye to the rest of the group. Then they came up the clearing towards us, accompanied by several others who were also planning to leave. Dilah was walking just behind them.

When the little group reached us, they began to say goodbye; almost as though it might be the last time they would see us. Most shook our hands, but some of them hugged us.

'What is this?' I wondered. 'Some kind of warm Kurdish social behaviour—or a contrived captor-captive bonding technique? Could it be a simple expression of genuine feeling? Perhaps it was the result of prayer.'

After they had left, Dilah told us the prime purpose of their mission. They were off, she said, to arrange for some Turkish journalists to be secretly transported to this mountain region, then brought blindfolded to our camp. Here they would be given the opportunity to meet us, the hostages, and see that we were all in good health and spirits. They would also be able to interview the guerrillas in our group first-hand. From them they would hear about the true plight of the Kurds, their fight for freedom and their demands for sovereignty.

These reporters, having been supplied all this information, along with photographs and video-recordings, would be blindfolded once more and escorted back to civilisation to break the story to the world.

I stared at Dilah in amazement.

'She's mad!' I thought. 'Perhaps this is the hare-brained plan she was already dreaming up when she said to us "It is not enough".'

Our simple suggestion to turn in a fair report on our captors may not have been enough; but this was too much! Did Dilah really believe that any rational reporter would risk his entire reputation and even his life by...

I was dumbfounded.

The plan was impossible—insane!

'If we are to be held here in these mountains until that happens,' I thought, 'we'll never be released.'

CHAPTER

8

If Winter Comes

Within three hours, everyone had left the campsite and moved to another mountain top. The new camp was at an even higher altitude than the last one. As we settled down to sleep it was noticeably colder.

Next morning our guard told us that tonight would be bath-night. He also said that Dilah's journalists would be with us in a day or so. The plan, no doubt, was that when these visitors met us they would be suitably impressed by our personal cleanliness and our freshly laundered clothes.

Although our guard seemed certain that the summit conference with the Press was definitely on, I was not quite so sure. The prospect of any self-respecting journalist being smuggled into such a highly militarised zone and then brought blindfolded to this mountain to do his interviews was absurd enough. But it would be pure fantasy to imagine that were he to survive all this personally, he would do so professionally after it was all over.

Crazy as the whole idea was, it did at least encourage them to give us our much longed-for bath-night.

Shortly after dark, Ablution Contingent Number One moved off. It consisted of Marvin, Gary and half a dozen guerrillas. They were gone for around four hours. When they returned, they were somewhat fatigued by what turned out to be an unexpectedly long trip, but were pleased to have washed themselves and their clothes. They told us that they had been an hour longer than expected because the group had become lost on its way back. I was rather glad I'd not volunteered to go in their contingent.

Ten minutes later, Richard, Ron and I, accompanied by another small group, were forcing our way through the scrub surrounding the camp and were headed for the *yayla*.

When we emerged from this scrub, we found ourselves on a high undulating plateau. It was stony, desolate and quite without vegetation, except for one grotesquely twisted tree just below the crest of the mountain ahead of us. We wended our way up the slope, past the tree and on around the mountain.

About forty minutes later, we began to descend into a bare and lonely valley. On its far side, nestling in amongst the rocky outcrops, were several flat-roofed stone buildings. They appeared to be almost part of the mountainside. So this was the *yayla*.

We went down into the valley where we crossed a stream and then began to climb up towards these very old, quite possibly ancient stone buildings which were vaguely reminiscent of the cliff dwellings built by North American Indians. Those who had built them had taken maximum structural advantage of the natural valley formation there. They had begun by choosing a reasonably wide flat rock shelf, then just back from its edge had

erected a long stone wall. This was to be the facade of the building. In this wall, they had left several gaps for doorways, but none for windows. Then running back at right-angles from the front wall to the rocky valley-side behind, they had built dividing walls to make rooms.

At various places inside the structure great logs had been erected as pillars to support the roof which was made of massive rafters covered with rocks and soil.

We ducked our heads and went inside. The place was filled with smoke which made breathing difficult. It stung my eyes. In a little adjoining room, I could see a small stove made from a round kerosene drum. On top of it a bowl of water was steaming.

The walls and rafters were blackened with the smoke of centuries. We took off our boots and socks. The mud floor felt wet and greasy underfoot, due no doubt to the exuberant bath-time splashings of Marvin and Gary. But beneath this slippery surface it was compacted and hard. I wondered how many feet had trodden it down to make it so.

One at a time we stripped off and began to wash our filthy bodies and clothes. When we had lathered ourselves with rough sand-soap, a young lad poured a basin of hot water over us. We dried ourselves then washed our clothes and hung them over the stove to dry them.

Within an hour we were dressed and ready to leave.

When every trace of our presence had been removed, we left the *yayla*. For some reason we headed back by a completely different route. After half an hour, unbelievably, we too ended up completely lost just as the first contingent had done. We wandered in the forest for well over an hour. Our meanderings might have gone on for much longer had a search-party from the camp not been sent out to find us.

As we eventually pushed our way back through the dense undergrowth near our camp-site I noticed that the slightest pressure on my left shin by branches and stems caused pain.

I had a look at it next morning in the daylight. It was swollen and inflamed but was nothing to worry about, I thought.

People busily came and went as they had done before, but today we heard no planes, helicopters or sounds of fighting.

We saw nothing of Ibrahim and very little of Dilah that day. However, the following morning, Dilah came over and initiated a conversation with us. She asked us whether we knew anything about the history of the Kurdish nation. We said we didn't know much about the subject; whereupon she immediately asked us whether we would like to have her tell us something about it. Not wishing to offend her, we said we would.

She slipped away and before long was back with a well-thumbed pamphlet in her hand.

She sat down on our rug and crossed her legs, as kindergarten teachers sometimes do when they are about to tell an interesting and exciting story to their children.

What Dilah began to share with us, her five pupils, we found moderately strong on interest, but decidedly weak on excitement. What she gave us was a laboriously slow word-for-word translation of the material in the pamphlet—from Kurdish, via her German, into our English. This first lesson took us back to the Indo-European origins of the Kurds and went on to trace their lineage from the ancient Hittites to the Medes. Dilah was anxious for us to understand that this noble nation to which she belonged had been persecuted for some 3,000 years.

It was already fairly obvious where she was heading. In later sessions she would move towards the current situation and the 'land rights' issue. Her goal would be to have us empathise with the Kurds as a people with no land of their own and no autonomous control over their political destinies. Her ultimate aim, I suspected, would be to bring us to the point where we would be not only sympathetic to the Kurdish cause, but even positively supportive of it. Perhaps, we might even become active supporters of the PKK and its efforts to achieve Kurdish sovereignty, particularly over Eastern Turkey.

Of course the five of us were already saddened by the plight of the Kurdish people. Like the rest of the world, we had watched in horror the media coverage of their terrible suffering in the wake of the Gulf War and Saddam Hussein.

In this sense we were perhaps potentially vulnerable to this gentle attempt to woo us politically. Our genuine concern for the Kurds, along with the accumulated physical and psychological stresses of our situation, might be just enough to make us succumb to Dilah's indoctrination.

This was certainly no crass brain-washing programme. No threat here of being endlessly interrogated and brow-beaten into alien beliefs, where the ultimate aim was to prop us up in front of some television camera to mouth hollow Marxist platitudes and deliver stony-faced apologies for having betrayed the workers of the world.

This was a friendly invitation to a group of men—most of them keen students of history—to consider some additional historical facts, to discuss them rationally and come to their own conclusions—voluntarily. The technique was difficult both to detect and deflect.

Had we been locked away somewhere and even beaten by our captors, we would have been angrier and perhaps more resistant to their beliefs, but Dilah's technique was simple, subtle and deadly dangerous.

How could we counter it?

Curiously enough, the answer to this question came without any conscious effort on our part.

Dilah's ideological sessions were countered; for example, by discussions amongst ourselves about our main archaeological text, the Old Testament. Although we did not have a copy to actually read, we knew it well enough to discuss it and its ideological implications. We examined several of its accounts, including the one about Abraham's attempt to sacrifice his son Isaac, and that of Joseph's life in Egypt.

There were other ways in which we were able to maintain our ideological integrity.

For example, the commitment of these guerrillas, as seen in the little morale-building ritual they held each evening, was balanced by our brief time of daily thanksgiving and prayer.

Their influence upon us was not only a matter of ideology and commitment. It also took other forms, each of which we balanced up in some way.

Vocationally, they did their everyday work as guerrillas; we did ours as we discussed our archaeological work.

Ethically, they were in general quietly courteous towards us; we were equally so towards them.

Culturally, they continued to keep their traditions alive by singing their Kurdish songs. We did likewise by singing our Western ones.

And so we were able to maintain our identity in these ways, which were like strands of a rope—woven together to form a life-

line that prevented us from drifting helplessly away to be
swamped in an ocean of political conformity.

Day after day, we waited for the promised arrival of our
journalist visitors.

They did not come.

Camp life continued much as it had done before, with perhaps
a couple of notable exceptions. Our diet was pleasantly widened.
It now occasionally included green peppers, lentil soup, yogurt
and a more interesting form of *ekmek* which had been baked with
cheese and butter. Our sleeping conditions were not so pleasant,
however. It was now much colder, and although we had been
given two large blankets this time, they were never adequate for
the five of us. No matter who shared which blanket with whom, it
never seemed to work out.

After several more days, the journalists had still not arrived.
This was our longest stay in any one place, which meant that we
no longer walked most nights as we'd been required to do before.
Night-time was once more sleeping time—at least the-
oretically—so we had more daytime opportunity to socialise.
This gave me a chance to talk with Ron about a number of
archaeological sites we had been researching in Israel, Egypt and
Saudi Arabia. He told me in some detail how in Saudi Arabia, he
and his two sons had been imprisoned and how worried he had
been as their father, because he'd felt responsible for having
allowed it to happen.

Occasionally, we swapped interesting stories. One day I
recited a selection of Australian and British poetry.

On the fourteenth day following our capture (the fourth on this
site), I realised that my leg was getting worse. The swelling had
increased and just below my calf I detected a hardening red
lump. I suspected that this lump might be a thrombosis. It was
painful and I had difficulty in walking. I spoke to Ron about it.
He said that in his opinion the inflammation indicated a condition known as phlebitis; that it was serious and certainly could
lead to the formation of a clot or thrombosis, as I had suspected.

'What can I do about it?' I asked.

'Stay off it and keep it up,' he answered.

'Will it improve if I do?' I asked.

'I doubt it,' he replied. 'You need medical attention—an anti-
coagulant.'

'Not much chance of getting that out here,' I said. 'I guess I'll just have to wait until we're released.'

'You need to get to a hospital so they can run tests on you to determine how much anti-coagulant you require,' Ron added.

I was glad of his free medical advice and immediately did the only thing possible; I lay down and propped my leg up in the fork of a sapling. Later that day, Marvin handed me a very respectable oak walking-stick which he had stripped, whittled and smoothed with his marvellous multi-purpose knife. I used this stick to reduce the risk of further swelling or clotting whenever I needed to walk.

After our lunch that day, Dilah noticed me hobbling back to my blanket under the trees. She said she had done two years of nursing back in Germany and asked if she could take a look at my leg.

As she did this, Ron, from across the clearing, said, 'It's phlebitis.'

I pointed to the tender lump below my calf. She pressed it very firmly—a procedure I did not greatly appreciate.

'He needs a doctor,' said Ron, articulating the words very slowly.

'It's bad,' he added. 'He needs a doctor.'

Dilah continued to look at my leg.

'The Professor needs drugs—"Coumadin",' he said.

Dilah looked at him and repeated the name.

Ron, holding her steadily in his gaze, said very slowly and deliberately: 'Coumadin must be prescribed by a *doctor*, in a *hospital*. The Professor must go to *hospital*,' he emphasised.

Dilah thought for a few moments then stood up and left us.

I suspected that right now she was adding Coumadin to the list of drugs she was planning to bring in from somewhere for her walking wounded.

'Ron,' I said, 'I don't think she understood what you said about my need of a doctor and a hospital.'

'Probably not,' he replied. 'In any case, I guess she reckons she's a medical expert 'cos she's done two years of nursing.'

'She probably knows about enough to make her dangerous,' I said. 'A blood-thinning agent like Coumadin could be risky to take without medical supervision, couldn't it?'

'It could kill yer,' he said.

I lay back and gazed up at the blue Turkish sky. I wondered how many guerrillas had been given drugs by medically unqualified people like Dilah and as a result had grown sicker and even died. I did not relish the thought of becoming such a casualty myself.

That night after dinner, before the fire had burned down, a number of the group gathered around and began to sing their Kurdish songs, most of which were patriotic and rousing. Others were rather mournful—musical laments bewailing the plight of the Kurdish people. All their songs were sung in unison and, while not rendered with refinement, were sung with considerable feeling and fervour.

Several times the men linked arms in a long line and began to dance as their onlookers clapped the rhythm. Their dances were not unlike those I had seen elsewhere in the Middle East, particularly in Israel.

When we five were invited to make our contribution to the programme, we sang a few songs in three-part harmony—passably well I thought. It was interesting to speculate how often, if ever, the craggy heights of the surrounding mountains had echoed to the strains of 'Amazing Grace', followed by a barbershop quartet rendering of 'Down by the Old Mill Stream'.

The next day, to our surprise, some of our guards came to us and requested an encore. These foundation members of our Freedom Fighters Fan Club put their request in the form of a question.

'*Sipping muzik?*' they asked. 'Sipping' was about as close as they could get to pronouncing the English word 'speaking'. In this quaint way they were asking whether we would speak music, or sing to them.

We indicated that we would sing something, then began to discuss what it might be.

I suggested the title of an old-time song which I thought we all should know. To my surprise, no-one could remember it.

'Surely you fellows know it,' I said. 'It goes like this'; whereupon I began to whistle the first line.

The result, to say the least, was extraordinary. The camp suddenly bristled with guns—most of them pointed in my direction. The clicks of their cocking mechanisms sounded like the finals of an international-speed typing competition.

There was also a good deal of frenzied shouting and scurrying for cover.

I sat there bewildered until I suddenly realised what I'd done. In guerrilla warfare all whistles are signals. Known ones are friendly; unknown ones hostile. My unfamiliar whistling had been interpreted as the signal of an encroaching enemy.

It had thrown the entire camp into full battle-stations alert.

I hardly ever whistle now.

Next day, Dilah stopped by to ask about my leg. The redness had begun to extend upwards from that lump along a vein. She could see that my condition was worsening, so I decided it was about time for me to put some psycho-political pressure on her.

I began by telling her that the lump was probably a clot. To make sure she understood, I used the Turkish word for clot which is *pıtı*. I had found it in Gary's Turkish-English dictionary, along with other words such as *hastane* which is 'hospital', *halp* which is 'heart' and *Olmek*, the word for 'die'. I was therefore able to tell her that if the clot moved to my heart, I would die. I hoped that being the political tactician she was, Dilah would realise how damaging to the PKK cause it would be should one of their hostages be denied medical attention and die on them.

Having gauged her response to my comments, I was fairly sure she had got the point. So I told her I wanted to see Ibrahim about the matter, hoping that in the light of all this, he might make a special effort to get me to a hospital and hopefully release the rest of our group at the same time. Dilah agreed to this, so I picked up my knobbly oak walking-stick and went down with her to Ibrahim's leafy little lair.

She told him in Kurdish what I had just told her. Ibrahim was finishing a cigarette. He watched her with those narrow eyes of his as she spoke. When she had finished, he drew deeply on his spent cigarette and flicked it away. Then he addressed me directly, puffing out the smoke of his last inhalation with each phrase.

'*Olmek,*' he said, with mock-seriousness.

'*Olmek, olmek,*' he said again in a cry-baby tone, this time using the fingers of both hands to mime the fall of tears from his eyes.

He was taunting me—chiding me for thinking I might die from a little leg problem. He chuckled quietly, as though inwardly enjoying the joke he'd just made at my expense, then took out another cigarette. Leaving it to wag loosely between his parted lips, he used both his hands to rummage for his lighter. He took it from his pocket and with one hand held it out from his mouth and flicked it. The end of his cigarette glowed a brightening red in the flame. As he leaned back and exhaled the smoke, I could see him mocking me with his narrow Mongolian eyes.

Within just five minutes, he had made me feel like a whingeing hypochondriac.

I was beginning to wonder why I'd even bothered to talk to the man. Taking my stick I made to leave. Then Ibrahim spoke to me in Kurdish with lots of gestures. He pointed to me, tapped his gun, then pointed to himself and then again to me. Dilah saw that I was not comprehending him, so she tried with her very limited English to translate.

'Ibrahim says, you, Professor—not be afraid.'

'Ibrahim says he have gun. Ibrahim says, you have Jesu Christ.'

I gathered from this that Ibrahim was assuring me I had no need to worry because he had the guns to control any threat to our physical lives and we Westerners had Jesus Christ to take care of our souls—and our spiritual lives.

Here was the Marxist materialist, the man of action, whose ultimate trust was in the god of the gun. As he reverently patted the stock of his automatic rifle he was paying homage to his god and avowing faith in him. If I had doubts about this god, or Ibrahim's effectiveness as a devout disciple of his, then I had only to call upon my God to make up the leeway.

After all, if Jesus Christ was God in the flesh, as we claimed him to be, wouldn't he be Lord of all things, visible and invisible, tangible and intangible—and wouldn't this include his care of my leg?

Ibrahim was not only testifying to faith in 'his' god, but, with almost evangelical fervour, was challenging me to have faith in 'mine'.

A theologian might perhaps say that his message was also ecumenical; a plea to fuse militant Marxism with Christianity—which is bottom-line liberation theology.

An Australian punter would probably say he was urging me to hedge my bets—or, in Aussie race-track slang, 'Have a bit each way'.

Simplistic as his comments first appeared to be, Ibrahim, with a few well-chosen words, had cleverly out-manoeuvred me. Suitably rebuked and chastened, I limped back to my rug and put my foot up. I went over in my mind the conversation I'd just had. I hadn't expected a lecture on theology, particularly from some Marxist ecumenical.

I had long been convinced that the Bible, if taken at its face value, does not endorse the modern-day ecumenical movement as it is currently espoused. There could be no marriage between Marxism and the biblical Christian faith. The liberation theologians were wrong—and so was Ibrahim. But then maybe he *was* right to rebuke me for not really trusting my God concerning this leg of mine. After all, the Bible does say in the Old Testament book of Proverbs 'Trust in the Lord with *all* thine heart and lean not to thine own understanding...'

Little did I realise how crucial this ancient piece of biblical advice was going to be to me as I faced the next few days.

That night we were told that the journalists would definitely be with us in the next day or two. So immediately following dinner, the entire camp, except for a young lad, a girl and myself, set out on another bath-night excursion to the *yayla*. We three remained behind, because it had been decided that I should not attempt the journey with my leg as it was.

The camp was deathly quiet. The three of us sat around the fire that had been used by the guerrillas further down the clearing. We talked for a while, then the young girl, whose name was Silan, began to sing. Her voice was husky but melodious. Although only around fourteen years of age, she handled with almost professional dexterity those tricky little quavers one hears in the vocal music of the Middle East. When I complimented her, she said that Dilah was a much better singer than she was.

The bath-night brigade returned around 10.30 pm. As they came into the clearing, I could see Richard was holding his right hand. On his way back, he had fallen and torn it on the edge of a stump. Dilah examined it and said she would get something for it. When it was time to go to sleep, I stayed where I was by the fire. Before she turned in, Dilah came over and sat down next to me. She told me that arrangements would shortly be made for me to take my bath here, adding that someone would be detailed to fetch the stove from the *yayla* so that water could be heated here at the camp.

Pointing to my leg, I raised the question again about a doctor and a *hastane*.

Her reply was somewhat evasive. She said that because of their busy guerrilla schedule, it would be difficult to co-ordinate.

As she stood up to leave, she suggested that I stay where I was by the fire to keep my leg warm.

The greying embers gave out very little heat, so I got as close to them as I could, then tried to get some sleep.

An hour or so later, I became aware of a quiet conversation between two people who were talking across the fire. Without opening my eyes I recognised the voices. One of these people was Silan, who had sung to me earlier in the evening, and the other was our articulate smooth-voiced gentleman; the goat butcher and adviser to Ibrahim. The tone of their conversation gradually became increasingly intimate—like the dialogue leading to a love scene in some foreign film.

After a while Silan went across and joined the man on the other side of the fire. Their voices became quieter. It was not necessary to understand what they were saying to know what was happening. I was deeply saddened by the thought that these vulnerable young girls had put themselves under the control of men who abused them in this way.

Next morning, as we were warming ourselves by the fire, there was a violent thrashing sound in the scrub nearby. It was followed by a shrill shrieking noise. Suddenly, a guerrilla burst out of the undergrowth, half-wrestling and half-trundling a wild-eyed goat. Another guerrilla slipped a noosed belt over the animal's head and tugged him, wriggling and kicking, towards a tree.

At breakfast, I could see that Richard was having trouble with the hand he had injured the night before. The ragged wound was already becoming infected. My leg was also a good deal worse. The redness around the calf had now extended up towards the inside of my knee. My entire lower leg was tender and swollen, the skin stretched over it with almost drum-hide tightness. Walking was now both painfully difficult and probably, I suspected, dangerous.

If I did have a clot, there was a distinct possibility that any strenuous activity might dislodge it and allow it to travel to my heart or lungs.

As Dilah walked by, Ron caught her attention and told her, as forcefully as he could, that unless I was given medical attention soon, I might actually die.

She gave him to understand that she was arranging for treatment. Ron stressed once again the importance of both a doctor and a hospital.

I followed that up by saying that, using my stick and the assistance of our small group, I was sure I could make it to a hospital. Ron countered my suggestion by saying that this would be too risky and that he, Marvin, Richard and Gary would carry me out. Characteristically, Marvin developed this idea by suggesting that a stretcher might be made from two poles and a rug. I had an embarrassing mental image of my four friends bearing me, shoulder-high serene and relaxed, down the mountain-side as they sweated and stumbled under my weight like the slaves of some ancient Middle-Eastern potentate.

My self-image as the dead-weight liability of the team was not improved when, after Dilah had left, I asked Çia for permission to visit the latrine. He looked at my boiler suit, face and hands and said,

'Professor, you are very dirty!'

As I made my painful way through the scrub, I saw the goat tied to his tree.

There he was, old and grey-bearded, dirty and evil-smelling and except for a few steps back and forth tied to the one spot.

I paused and patted him on the head.

'Know just how you feel old fellow,' I said, suppressing the additional thought that he might not be long for this world.

The morning grew very hot, so we all escaped into the shade. I was lying on my rug with my ankle up. The others had been given a pack of cards by the guerrillas and were playing a game of four-handed poker across the clearing. Dilah appeared and went across to them. She gave Richard a tube of anti-biotic cream for his hand. Then she came over to me and gave me a little square box of tablets. They contained Coumadin. I had requested medical treatment and here it was; Dilah's do-it-yourself remedy for venous thrombosis. Just as I had thought she might, she had conveniently ignored Ron's warning that this drug must be prescribed only by a doctor who knows from special tests how much a particular patient needs. I hoped she wouldn't stay around to make sure I took it, having gone to so much trouble to get it for me.

I quickly thanked her. To my relief, she hurried away to attend to something else.

In Shakespeare's *Romeo and Juliet* there is a scene where Juliet, to avoid having to marry a man she doesn't love, is given by a kindly friar a potion which will put her into a death-like trance. Juliet, at the moment when she is to drink the potion from its vial, is suddenly traumatised by a terrible thought. Is the liquid a sleep-inducing mixture, through which she will be able to escape a fate worse than death—marriage to the wrong man? Or is it, as Shakespeare has her ask,

> '. . Poison, which the friar
> Subtly hath minister'd to have me dead?' (IV.iii).

Like poor Juliet, I really didn't know whether the prescription I was supposed to take would solve my problem—or simply kill me. To be sure, I urgently needed the right amount of medication to stop my blood from coagulating into life-threatening clots, but I had no idea of what the right amount was. If I took too much, I could find myself developing internal haemorrhages in dangerous places and become a sort of chemically-induced haemophiliac.

As Ron said, 'It can kill yer.'

On this particular day, I may have looked and felt like a silly old goat, but I had no intention of acting like one. So I shoved the packet into my pocket and left it there—unopened.

Later that day, we decided we'd try to make our sleeping conditions a little more bearable. The guards allowed us to borrow a shovel which we used to level out and soften the hard sloping surfaces where we'd been trying to sleep. Having done this, we strewed them with leaves. Our guards also let us have some empty plastic bags which we stuffed full of leaves to make pillows.

We were still involved in these activities when I was told it was time for my bath.

I was taken up the slope and through the main guerrilla sleeping area to a place a little further on among the trees. Here was a kerosene tin filled with piping hot water. There was also a basin, towel, soap—and luxury of luxuries!—a plastic bottle of shampoo. To ensure that I could bathe in privacy, a rug was hung between two trees as a screen.

After I had washed myself, I washed my clothes and draped them over some bushes where they soon dried in the warm afternoon sun.

Feeling considerably refreshed, I dressed, took up my stick and started back with my guard. On our way through the guerrilla area again, I noticed Ibrahim. I stopped to have a word with him. He told me he was making plans to get me down from the mountains and into a hospital—on a donkey, he said.

I took this as I'd learned to take many other promises made about our release—with a grain of salt.

During my absence, the goat had been slaughtered and was now in the process of becoming the meat supplement for our evening meal. When that meal was served, we found it to be one of the most varied we had eaten. Along with the goat meat, a number of other dishes were served, including, to Ron's delight, several slices of *karpuz* or water-melon.

Marvin was predictably the most delighted of all of us with this meal, since he was able to indulge his passion for goat-liver again. Barely half an hour later, after he'd eaten copious quantities, he began to get severe stomach pains and was violently ill. As much as I was sorry to see the poor chap suffer in this way, I did hope he would profit from the experience, and forsake his morbid predilection for animal organs.

That evening there was more singing and dancing. In spite of her reticence, Dilah was persuaded to sing for us. She had a fine voice and knew how to use it. She sang a sad song about the snow-covered mountains of Kurdistan. As I listened, I could not help but think how that lovely voice could be silenced forever by a single bullet—obscenely snuffed out by that wanton wastrel, war.

That night marked the close of a generally sad day. The unresolved nature of our situation was frustrating. Some of us were starting to show signs of cracking physically as well. As we turned in, Marvin was still very nauseated; Richard's hand was throbbing and the infection was spreading; and my leg was noticeably worse.

The following day was to prove to be even more difficult.

The night having been achingly cold and largely sleepless, none of us was in a frame of mind to take another of Dilah's history lessons when she arrived that morning with her pamphlet.

The topic was modern Kurdish history and Dilah, the Marxist ideologue, was soon in full flight. She dilated upon the evils of imperialism and its suppression of the Kurdish people, then extolled the virtues of communism as the only effective antidote for them.

She rejected the suggestion that some of us made, that communism could no longer be considered effective in the light of its recent collapse in the USSR and several other countries. She seemed to be saying that the collapse of this wonderful political system had been calculatingly precipitated by the imperialist West—notably by the power barons of the United States of America.

Dilah's assertion did not go down well with us, the members of her class—especially those who were American. They pointed out that the United States had for many years provided huge amounts of foreign aid to Russia and other ailing nations behind the Iron Curtain. The point was also strongly made that America and several other so-called 'imperialist' nations had stood up to Saddam Hussein in the Gulf War, condemning in particular his vicious treatment of the Kurds. They pressed home their point even further by saying that following that war, huge amounts of food and clothing were dropped from United States helicopters to the Kurdish refugees who had been herded by Hussein up into the bleak mountains on the border of Iraq and Turkey.

Dilah denied the truth of this. 'Not so!' she expostulated— abandoning her usual self-control. 'I was there!'

A raw nerve had been touched. The pupils had challenged their teacher and the class was in danger of turning into a ideological uproar.

We all sensed it was time to pull back.

If part of Dilah's aim was to win us to her cause, then this rebuff might make her reconsider the wisdom of the mooted plan to release us. At the moment, it seemed likely that we might not be eligible for early release for good behaviour. It was even more possible that Commandant Dilah might already have evaluated our current state of mind and heart and decided once more: 'It is not enough.'

If so, she might even now, be considering the possibility of enrolling us in an extended remedial course in Kurdish history.

Even after Dilah had departed, our annoyance did not dissipate. The five of us discussed the possibility that Dilah, in clinging to the hope that her reporters might yet come, might have put pressure on Ibrahim to stay here in the one place. We wondered whether we might in fact have been released earlier if Dilah had not arrived on the scene.

Her doctrinaire teaching, together with the general situation, had filled us with a simmering mixture of despondency and annoyance. These feelings were beginning to boil over and we vented them, perhaps rather unjustly, on Dilah. For Richard, emotions ran even higher when later in the morning he became embroiled in a verbal skirmish with Çia. As I lay immobilised with my leg propped up, I heard Richard telling Çia that we simply had to be released. He stressed the fact that we were longing to see our families and that they needed us.

Çia responded to this plea with the utmost earnestness. 'Richard, our Kurdish families suffer also. Everywhere they suffer.' Then brilliantly moving to the level of ideological generalisation, he added, 'Oppressed people suffer in Kurdistan, Lebanon, Palestine, Iraq...' His final thrust was to call on all who would desire to liberate the oppressed peoples of the world—Richard included, of course—to make the necessary sacrifices.

'We must all suffer to make them free. You too must suffer, Richard!'

As Richard continued to argue with him, I caught his eye and, frowning, shook my head as if to say, 'Don't pursue it further.'

We five had come from countries where there were laws protecting freedom of speech and the expression of personal opinion. But as hostages in the Middle East, we did not have the protection of such laws. To speak up as though we did was to invite a negative reaction and even reprisals.

Richard took my hint and the conversation came to an abrupt close. He joined me on my rug where we talked together for the next half hour.

Just before lunch I noticed that the others were examining a photograph that was being shown them by one of the guards.

Richard and I both went to look at it. It showed a group of guerrillas, both male and female, some standing, others crouching, all with guns and all rugged up in heavy coats and scarves. The photograph had been taken in winter. The mountains were blanketed in deep snow and the oak trees were quite bare. I recognised several of the people in the group. I asked the guard how they could possibly have survived such low temperatures.

He mimed the act of digging, and the shape of a house.

'*Bir oda?...kar?*' I asked, to check that I had understood his mime correctly: a room made of snow.

He nodded with a smile.

With no foliage to hide them, he and his comrades would be easily seen from the air. So throughout winter, they lived in the snow, or under it—in igloos.

Those who were part-time summer recruits would return to their homes and stay there for the winter. But permanent full-timers could never do this. They were the igloo-dwellers, hiding in the mountains, all of them exiled in their own land, all of them banished for ever from their homes.

We were nearing the end of summer now. The nights were already bitterly cold. I looked at the oak trees that arched overhead. Their leaves were already turning gold. Soon they would begin to fall.

The snow would come and winter would be suddenly upon us.

Would we still be here, living in igloos too perhaps?

Marvin was still too ill to share lunch with us. He lay down quietly in the shade and rested. Early in the afternoon the temperature dropped, the sky became overcast and rain began to fall—the first since we'd been captured. As it started to get heavier, we erected a makeshift tent with our blankets and huddled together under it.

The guerrillas simply went about their usual business, unperturbed by the rain. The downpour continued for well over an hour, by which time our blankets were sopping wet and dripping all over us. By the time the rain had cleared, we, our clothes and the blankets we needed to keep us warm that night were drenched.

We set about drying ourselves beside two roaring fires that had been specially lit for the purpose. In half an hour our clothes were almost dry. Our blankets however posed a much greater problem. They were so laden with water that we had to support them on stout poles. The guerrillas patiently assisted us in all this. For the first hour, our blankets steamed like saunas and it was not until another hour had elapsed that they began to show signs of drying. Then of course, the problem was to prevent them from catching fire in the flames.

Although we did the best we could, it was soon clear that our blankets would still be damp and dank by bed-time.

Our captors did not seem to have any such problems. They had stacked all their blankets in heaps under plastic bags and capes as soon as the rain began. Unlike us, they did not fight the elements. They co-operated with them. After a heavy afternoon's work, they had all enjoyed an invigorating shower and tonight would be ready to snuggle up into warm blankets for a good night's sleep. Our attempt to cope with the rain had cast serious doubt on the widely-held notion of Western superiority.

Little that had happened during the day had given us much cause to rejoice. By late afternoon, we were beginning to feel rather disconsolate and depressed. Suddenly, we were told that we would all be released—'tonight'!

We were to be led down from the mountains to a pre-arranged point, where a car would be waiting to take us on to a town. There we would be released, and I could be treated in a hospital. I would be taken down, as we had been told earlier, on a donkey, they said.

While we wanted to believe we were really leaving, our response to this news was restrained. Would this turn out to be another failed promise? Those who served us dinner seemed to think it was genuine. One of them pointed to me and said, '*Hastane*, Professor—*Hastane*!'

Having no luggage to pack, all we needed to do was wait for night to fall.

So we waited.

When it was dark, there was no sign of the promised exodus.

However we continued to wait, in the hope that we might simply be making a late start. By 10.30, we were still there, seated around a fire which, like our hopes for release, was slowly dying. We could hear a conversation going on down in Ibrahim's headquarters. Eventually a guerrilla came up and told us to go to bed, because due to 'certain problems' we would not be leaving.

Although we were not told what the problems were, they were not hard to imagine. The major one was the presence of the Turkish military. In spite of the report we had heard to the contrary, I was quite sure that the search for us was continuing. If that were so, then these guerrillas still had thousands of Turkish troops breathing down their necks and waiting, guns poised, for their next move. Under those circumstances, getting five men down out of these mountains without being killed would be close to impossible. Taking hostages is comparatively easy, since the hostage-taker can choose his time and place. But getting them back is quite another matter.

For this group, it was also a race against time. If we were not released very soon, the world would begin to presume us dead and this would be highly damaging to the PKK cause. If any of us should be killed, or die (as could possibly happen in my case) the political repercussions for them would be equally disastrous.

And now, to complicate matters even more, winter was virtually upon us. We had had the problem of rain today, but tomorrow it might be snow.

The game was almost up; we were rapidly approaching a stalemate. But worse than that, one false move might bring an angry outburst that could wipe all the pieces right off the board. Although we did not discuss these matters, I knew they would be echoing through the minds of the others. Richard became quite angry. He was particularly concerned for my well-being. Looking me straight in the eye across the fire, he said,

'Dr Roberts, Ah'm gonna git yew out o' here if Ah hev t' carry yew out mahself!'

'It's OK, Richard,' I said, in an attempt to placate him. 'I'll be all right. Let's get some sleep now.'

The rest of us got up to go to bed, but Richard sat right where he was, sullenly hunched over the shrunken heap of dead ashes that had earlier been a fire. Our guard stood behind him, his gun held diagonally across his chest.

'Come to bed, Richard,' Marvin said firmly.

'Ah'm not goin' t' bed!' he mumbled, staring straight ahead.

'Yew sit there any longer,' said Ron, 'an' yew'r gonna git a gun-butt in yew'r skull.'

After a few seconds of tense silence, Richard stood up and came across to us.

We'd all had enough. No matter what these guerrillas said, there was never any way of knowing whether they were telling the truth.

As we settled down for the night the ground under us was wet, our blankets were damp and the temperature was already close to freezing...

The next morning we were awakened to an unmistakable sound—the 'hee-haw' of a donkey!

CHAPTER
9
The Plan For Our Release

I'd never ridden a donkey before. But I was highly motivated to learn as I hobbled with my stick to the end of the column.

As we stood there, Dilah emerged to bid us farewell. How does one say goodbye to one's hostages—especially when they have rejected one's indoctrination? She was almost regally formal as she moved along the column to each of us and shook our hands. After Dilah had said goodbye (not, I was pleased to note, *'Auf Wiedersehen'*), we were ready to leave.

Suddenly, out from the undergrowth where he had been tethered since that morning, came my little four-legged ambulance.

How tiny he was. Could that frail little body support the weight of a grown man? And those slim delicate legs with their dainty fetlocks—would they not snap under the strain?

The man who was leading him by a rope halter threw a folded rug over his little grey back, then, patting it with one hand, motioned me with the other to mount the animal; an action more like swinging one's leg over a bicycle seat then mounting a steed. The man, who was to double as both my donkey keeper and my guard, took my stick under his arm and helped me 'on' rather than 'up' since, once seated, my feet almost touched the ground.

The column moved off; my guard, the donkey and myself bringing up the rear.

Here I was, on these wild mountainous heights, in the golden glow of a Middle-Eastern sunset—riding on a donkey. By so doing, I was joining the ranks of those, who down through history, had ridden on donkeys: author G.K. Chesterton in the south of France; the virgin Mary, if Bible picture books are to be believed; and that famous film star Nelson Eddy, in *Donkey's Serenade*.

I also recalled one of our ANZAC servicemen, John Simpson Kirkpatrick, who when Australia was fighting Turkey at Gallipoli in 1915 brought injured Australians down from the heights there on a donkey. I chuckled to myself. This evening, the injured Australian descending from these Turkish heights on a donkey was being brought down by a Kurdish Turk.

Riding a donkey is not as easy as it looks; particularly if one is going down a steep-sided mountain. When the animal is headed downwards, one's natural tendency is to lean forward and at times even to hang on to his neck. Of course the correct way is to sit back on the curve of his rump; then, when his body assumes a downhill attitude, lean backwards.

This sure-footed little animal picked his way down between and over the rocky outcrops with nonchalant skill. Whenever he had to negotiate a steep ledge, his head would suddenly go down and I would know at once that I had to lean back to retain my balance. Then, as he jumped down and became horizontal again, I would have to return quickly to my perpendicular position. After a while, when I had somewhat gained my confidence, I stopped gripping his sides tightly with my knees and let my legs hang down loosely, which I found actually helped me balance myself.

I felt I was just beginning to get the hang of it when the little beast decided (rather over-ambitiously, I thought) to jump down from a quite high ledge. He landed awkwardly and stumbled on some loose rocks. Since there were no girth-straps to hold anything in place, I and the blanket slipped off on to the rocks— fortunately on to my good right leg. While it would not be technically accurate to say I 'dismounted', I deny emphatically that I was thrown!

The track ahead was even rougher, so my guard gave me back my stick, readjusted the donkey's blanket, then led him falteringly down over the jumble of rocks. Using my stick, I did my best to keep up. After a quarter of a mile or so, the track levelled out again and I was invited to remount.

It was a clear night. The blue-black sky was studded with bright stars. The valley into which we were descending was wide and craggy—wild and beautiful, even at night. I thought how impressive it would be in daylight.

Looking down the track over the nodding head of my long-eared little companion, I could just make out the rest of our group; small shadowy figures on the steep side of the valley.

We continued on for another half-hour or so, by which time I estimated we had come down well over a thousand feet from our camp-site.

Soon the track became so rocky and steep again that my donkey began to hesitate and needed coaxing. So my guard made me continue once more on foot. At the bottom of this rocky section, we rounded a bend and found the rest of the group there resting at the side of the track. A few minutes later, we moved on again. The track was wider now, large enough to take a horse-drawn vehicle. We'd gone only a few hundred yards when our leader stopped abruptly and raised his hand. Then he turned to face us and held both his hands up in a 'don't move an inch' gesture and signalled silence with a forefinger to his lips.

I slipped quietly down from the donkey and joined the column. Everybody stood absolutely motionless.

Except for a stunted thorny tree on the edge of the road, there was no cover in sight. Militarily we were in a highly vulnerable situation, an easy target for troops anywhere in the area, particularly if they were across that valley. To anyone over there we must have looked like a cast of actors at centre stage frozen in tableau for a press photograph, or about to line up for a curtain call—our backdrop the bare mountain slope behind, and our orchestra-pit the valley that dropped steeply away from the road.

The vital question was, 'Where is the audience tonight?'— across the valley, above us on the mountain top, or hiding below the level of the road among the boulders?

None of us moved a muscle for ten minutes. The only sound was that of a hungry donkey tearing tufts of grass from the edge of the road and munching them.

The leader of our group sent off two men to reconnoitre. Another man took the donkey away, probably to his owner somewhere in the valley. The leader lowered himself into a comfortable squatting position and the rest of us followed his example. Still nobody spoke and nobody moved. We remained there for a whole hour.

When the scouts returned, they whispered a few words to the leader who immediately gave the signal to move on down the road. This the column did at a very brisk pace. They were obviously in a great hurry now, perhaps because of the danger of the situation, or perhaps to make our rendezvous with the car at the appointed time.

My guard held me by my left arm to take some of the weight from my left leg and to ensure that I kept up with those ahead. As he forced me along, I found it necessary to take large paces. I tried to use my stick to soften the jarring impact of each step as my left leg pounded against the road. After about two miles, my leg was throbbing and the pain in my calf had become intense.

If I did have a venous thrombosis, there was little doubt that this kind of rough treatment could well dislodge it and cause it to move through my bloodstream, with fatal results. I began to consider the unpleasant possibility that fragments of it might have been dislodged already. If that were the case, then any step I took could be my last.

I decided it was the right time to pray. So I put the whole situation in the hands of a God who, having created this body of mine, knew far more about it than I or any doctor could know. I asked that the ultimate outcome, regardless of what might happen to me personally, would be for his best.

Then I thanked him for it and began to sing in my mind a Christian chorus I had learned in England:

Give thanks with a grateful heart,
Give thanks to the Holy one,
Give thanks because he's given
Jesus Christ his Son...

I kept singing these words, to the painful rhythm of my pounding stride.

Another two miles' march brought us to the head of the valley. Down to our left, below the level of the road, I could hear the steady flow of a small river. To our right the side of the valley was now a high canyon wall. And just a little way ahead, the road skirted around the semi-circular base of a gigantic limestone outcrop that towered a thousand feet above us. Just beyond this spectacular formation a silver cascade tumbled from a gully in the side of the valley. Its multi-stranded waters raced erratically down a long rocky incline where they splashed and swirled around impeding rocks and logs; then, scurrying down between boulders and through crevices, ultimately emerged as a quiet ford gently lapping across the road.

The man in charge of our group was about to lead us across to the other side, when several guerrillas emerged from behind boulders there. By the time we had all forded the stream, there were nine or ten guerrillas waiting to greet us.

When we had quenched our thirst, we stretched out on the rock shelves bordering the road. I propped my leg up on a rock to relieve the pain. We waited here for almost an hour. I wondered where our car was, so I decided to ask.

'*Araba, nerede?*'

I did not get an answer. After half an hour had elapsed, it became fairly apparent that the car wasn't coming. We would not be transported out tonight.

It was around eleven o'clock when we were made to form up once more into our column and were marched up through the forest to the new group's campsite. This was situated in a tiny clearing on the top of a mountain, overlooking the valley through which we had just come. On reaching the summit, I estimated that we had climbed six or seven hundred feet since we had left the road. It had been a very steep and hard climb too. I found it particularly so, and was glad of the assistance given to me by one of the young men of the new group.

At the campsite, we were introduced to the leader. His name was Kocak. He was taller than most Kurdish males, very athletic and quite striking in appearance. He wore a heavy black beard. When we were introduced to him, he responded with an affable smile and firm handshake. He wore no jacket and his khaki trousers were supported by a stout pair of braces. I reckoned he was around thirty years of age.

There were also several women in the group. Two of them introduced themselves as archaeology students enrolled at a university in Ankara. They said that they had discontinued their studies to complete a period of service with this Kurdish self-styled 'national' army, the PKK.

It was very late, and time to retire. None of us had blankets or coverings of any kind as we lay down to sleep.

I found a place on the edge of the clearing and curled up there, just a few feet away from Marvin and Gary. Ron and Richard settled down in the middle of the clearing. We were all very tired and quickly began to go to sleep.

So began the most unpleasant night of my life.

I awoke within an hour, aching with cold. I stood up and tried to warm myself by vigorously moving and rubbing my limbs. Even after doing this continuously for ten minutes, my legs were still cold and numb. This was particularly the case with my left leg, where the circulation had already been so seriously impaired. I had lost a good deal of my body heat and knew that I could easily be a candidate for frostbite, or, if the temperature continued to drop, hypothermia.

I resolved therefore to stay on my feet and continue to move and massage my legs—if necessary, for the rest of the night.

I noticed, as I glanced up to the spot where Ron and Richard had lain down, that they had somehow managed to borrow a large waterproof cape—like a Mexican-style poncho with a head-hole and a hood. They were both asleep under it, as far as I could tell. I was interested to know how the rascals got such preferential treatment.

I looked across at Marvin and Gary. Gary was having similar problems to my own. He was massaging the calves of both legs. As for Marvin, he was of course sound asleep; comfortably curled up on his side, in his usual somnolent posture—both knees together and his head pillowed on his bent arm.

'Come over with us and share some body heat,' said Gary. Marvin stirred as Gary spoke, then added, 'C'mon over, Al.'

I knew that their suggestion was a wise one. Hot coals, if separated and spread, soon lose their heat; but if kept together, retain it. The same principle applied here.

'Get in between us and warm up for a bit,' said Marvin, leaving room for me between Gary and himself.

After ten minutes I could feel myself starting to warm up on both sides, like a piece of bread in an electric toaster. However, within another twenty minutes, Gary was beginning to freeze in front and Marvin was freezing behind. It was time to change positions. I went to the front, Gary to the back and Marvin warmed up between us. We swapped around in this way every half-hour for the next five hours, in an effort jointly to conserve our thermal resources.

Ultimately of course, the air-temperature at this high altitude began to take its toll. By about 4.30 am, I could not lie still without shivering, so I stood up and started again to rub my hands and legs. Both Gary and Marvin from time to time did the same. I also took the risk of stamping my feet to stimulate my circulation, even though I knew it might dislodge a blood clot.

All the guerrillas were wrapped up in their blankets. Though they were probably not really warm, they did not appear to be affected as badly by the cold as were Marvin, Gary and myself. I could not see Ron and Richard at all, since they were totally covered by their poncho. However, as they were quite motionless, I assumed they were asleep.

I shall never forget the agony of the next hour as I walked back and forth desperately trying to stay warm, longing for the sun to rise. Nor shall I forget when it finally did; how we stood by the fire as soon as it was lit, and luxuriated in its wonderful warmth.

After a very basic breakfast of *ekmek* and *çay*, the five of us curled up and went to sleep.

After lunch, dark blue-grey clouds began to gather around the mountaintops. Then it turned cold, and rain began to fall. This time, having no blankets under which to sit, Marvin, Gary and I moved in with Ron and Richard who let us sit under their poncho. As before, the guerrillas became saturated while completing their chores, but simply dried off around the fire when the weather improved.

As Kocak stood with clouds of steam rising from his body, he began to make conversation. He told us about his grandfather's religious beliefs, first by miming the horns of a cow then mooing and adding the name 'India'. All of this told us that his grandfather worshipped the sacred cow. Next, he pointed to the fire, then to the sun, and put his palms together to suggest the act of worship.

'Ron,' I said, 'these are the elements of ancient Babylonian worship.'

'Nimrod is still around on these mountains,' said Ron.

I was fascinated to find that Baal-worship of the bull and the sun had survived into the twentieth century and still existed here, in the very region where it may have originated.

As soon as the guerrillas were dry again, they linked arms and danced around the fire. Was this a kind of spontaneous celebration of the fact that the sun had driven away the rain—a sort of rain dance in reverse?

When it began to get dark, preparations to leave began.

The tops of the mountains were wreathed in misty rain. It promised to be another very cold night. Coats were donned and buttoned or zipped. Collars and hoods were pulled up. A man was winding a silken cummerbund around his waist; a very effective part of one's attire for keeping the loins warm.

While we stood waiting to leave and meet our car, Kocak glanced up at the lowering sky. He mimed with fluttering fingers the fall of snow.

'*Kar?*' I asked, using the Turkish word for snow.

He nodded, then stretching his arm high above his head, extended his hand forward horizontally and said,

'*Uç metre.*'

'How could you even walk here on these mountains, if they were covered with almost ten feet of snow?' I asked him, miming my question.

By way of reply, he outlined the shape of snow-shoes with his hands and demonstrated their function with the tramp of his feet.

I could not help but be impressed by his quiet pragmatism—if the snow is too deep to walk *through*, then walk *on* it with snow-shoes. The appalling difficulty and discomfort of it all obviously did not bother him in the slightest. Like most of his countrymen, he bore the privations of winter with cheerful resignation.

How different are the Kurds, I thought again, to those of us who live in the Western world. We are so mindful of our physical well-being and comfort. If we are threatened by the cold, we put on our expensive winter clothes or turn up our costly central-heating.

But the Kurds, having neither our financial resources nor our self-indulgent attitudes, stoically brave the cold—shivering and freezing, but content with the thought that it will be warm tomorrow; and if not tomorrow, perhaps the next day or some time after that. For centuries, while we have lived in the lap of luxury, they have barely survived on the edge of privation and disaster. I could not help but think what a formidable enemy they constituted for any government they opposed in guerrilla warfare.

I knew that Kocak and his little band were undaunted by the prospect of another freezing night on this mountain. But as for my friends and myself, that car could not come soon enough.

It was time to leave. Each of us took his place between two guards in the column. Then, with Kocak in the lead, we set off down the mountain.

A few hundred yards along the narrow mountain track we came to a small clearing. Here Kocak stopped us.

He walked back along the column, and without a word, took each of us by the arm. He made us stand together in our own little line, several yards away from the others and parallel to them.

We stood there, the five of us, facing the guerrillas.

Kocak gave an order. His group came to attention.

'There's never been anything like this since our capture,' I thought. 'What's going on?'

Kocak gave another order which brought all the guns up at forty-five degrees.

Then he made them number off: '*Yek, de, se, car...*'

As a researcher I had tried over the years to start with verified facts. Then I'd sought to interpret them in the most reasonable way, to come to a correct conclusion—rationally, not emotionally.

The facts of this situation needed little verification. The five of us had been taken into the bush and stood up in front of a line of guerrillas, who had been called to attention by their leader and were now facing us with their guns at the ready.

My interpretation of these facts came suddenly, as a frightening thought that ricocheted crazily about inside my mind.

An emotional and wild thought to be sure; I tried to suppress it—unsuccessfully, for I knew that it tallied all too well with the facts of the moment.

This was a firing squad!

CHAPTER
10
Release

Something had gone terribly wrong.
They'd probably just found out that in spite of their plans, there was now no prospect of getting us out—and they had decided to kill us. They'd probably explain it to the world by saying we'd been shot while trying to escape.

Kocak spoke to the group again.

Was this the part where the guns would come up and be aimed at us?

Suddenly, something unexpected happened.

The guerrillas facing us chorused a response to what Kocak had just said to them.

Kocak spoke again.

They chorused back again.

This was no firing squad! Kocak was leading his group through one of their guerrilla morale-building rituals!

'Of course!' I thought. 'Kocak has stopped them here to hold it on the way down from the mountain—and since these little rituals are always closed sessions for PKK personnel alone, we five had to be removed from the column before the questions and responses began!'

I had completely misinterpreted the situation. I felt a mixture of foolishness and relief. Had the others thought and felt the things I had in those few frightening moments? Had they been victims of their own free-wheeling imaginations too?

I was too embarrassed to ask.

We rejoined the column and continued on our way down through the forest. I wondered if Kocak had any idea of the mental and emotional upheaval he'd just put me, and perhaps my friends, through.

As I pressed on, stick in hand and assisted by one of the guards, I turned the situation over in my mind. I realised I'd been foolish even to entertain the possibility that we were about to be shot. Everything that had happened since we'd been prisoners indicated that killing us was simply not an option for those who'd taken us. While there was always the danger of a confrontation in which we and the others could be killed, it was highly unlikely that any of the guerrillas would choose to shoot us. For Kocak or any one else, to do it or allow it would be to put their own lives in jeopardy with the PKK High Command or political arm.

The whole thing had shown me how vulnerable I was. I had imagined I was in control. But this weird little experience had indicated very forcefully that under the pressure of the moment, one can totally misread a situation and jump to foolish conclusions—perhaps, even embark upon equally foolish actions.

As we came down the mountain, we retraced our previous evening's climb. When we reached the bottom, we were made to wait in the forest a hundred yards or so short of the road. The guerrillas who had accompanied us to this new site shook our hands and departed. No doubt they were heading off to rejoin Ibrahim's and Dilah's group, wherever they were encamped now.

Most of Kocak's group left us also, although Kocak himself, along with half a dozen others, stayed—no doubt to watch out for the car and to ensure, when it came, that we were all safely in it and away.

It was still very wet underfoot, so we stood quietly around waiting and listening for the car.

Although it was only 6.30 pm, the evening had already grown very cold and we began to walk about to offset its numbing effects. I noticed a stinging sensation in my toes, especially those of my left foot. In spite of Marvin's splendid repair job, my bargain boots were not waterproof and hadn't been for many days. As a result of the afternoon's rain, my feet and socks had been saturated for several hours. I suspected that the temperature of the water in contact with my feet and constantly seeping into my boots was close to freezing.

I went across to one of our guards, and pointing to my watch, asked him, '*Araba ne zaman?*'

'*Sekiz de*' he replied.

'The car's coming at eight,' I said to Marvin. 'We've got to wait another hour and a half.'

So we waited.

Two hours later, there was still no car. Would it come at all?

The possibility that we might have to spend yet another night here, without blankets, was too devastating to contemplate.

Kocak decided that it was time for us to have some supper. So to get the water for our *çay*, everyone except those keeping vigil for the car went down to the cascade near the road. Before we had time to boil our water, one of the men we'd left behind suddenly arrived with the news that the car had just come. Immediately, we made our way back along the road. And there it was, parked under the trees; a white Renault 16.

One of the guerrillas took some rolled-up *ekmek* from his haversack and handed it around. We ate it quickly. It brought to my mind how the Children of Israel, before their exodus from Egypt, ate their meal 'in haste'. Here we were, just before our release, eating unleavened bread, exactly as they did. I hoped that the man in charge of us would not change his mind as Pharaoh did, and try to bring us back into captivity once our exodus was underway.

When supper was over, we handed back the jackets our captors had lent us and crowded into the car. Ron, Marvin and Richard sat in the back and Gary and I crammed into the front with the driver.

I am told that policemen who road-test candidates for their driving licences can tell a great deal about their driving ability from the way they reverse their vehicles. Our driver lit a cigarette and engaged reverse gear with a shuddering 'chonk'; then, engine still racing, bumped backwards over the rough ground. By the time he had noisily shifted into first gear and was heading for the road, I had more or less completed my assessment of his competence as a driver.

His poor little car, woefully underpowered and mercilessly

overloaded, flounced angrily on to the gravelly surface and, roaring out its resentment, moved sullenly and slowly up the slope.

I sensed we were in for a very interesting drive.

Our driver was a middle-aged man with a thick moustache and stubbly face. He was a passionate individual, a volatile character who did everything with rugged verve. He drove like a rally driver and played the raucous PKK music on his cassette in the same way—flat out.

We gained altitude quickly and were soon nearing the top of the range. How strange it was to view the road ahead and involuntarily estimate how far and how long we'd have to walk— and then find that we were covering the distance in a matter of minutes. The experience was dream-like, unreal, as though we'd stepped magically forward into the twentieth century again.

We were now high in the clouds and rain began to fall. As it became heavier we wound the windows up. Our driver struck up a conversation. To make himself heard above the drumming of the rain, the roaring of the engine and the blaring of his music, he had to shout.

'*PKK tammum*, huh?' he yelled in his burly voice.

'*Tammum*,' I answered. There was no point in saying anything derogatory about the PKK at this stage. Then, diverting the conversation away from the risky topic of politics into the relatively safe one of food, I added,

'*Buyuk ekmek, buyuk domates, çorba ve çay—ve karpuz!*'

Having listed some of the items on our menu, I then told him that they were very good.

'*Çok guzel,*' I said.

'*Çok guzel,*' he repeated with obvious satisfaction, holding up his left hand, forefinger and thumb touching and little finger crooked.

We bumped and splashed our way through streams and puddles. Broad sheets of water covered much of the road. As we drove through them, the water drummed and reverberated beneath our feet, slightly retarding our forward movement.

Our driver was unperturbed by these less than ideal conditions and continued to accelerate, brake and swerve around corners as though he were hot favourite in the Grand Prix. The possibility that we might skid over the edge of this narrow road, to plunge or roll hundreds of feet into the valley, seemed not to occur to him.

I tapped Gary on the knee.

'Enjoying the drive?' I asked him.

'Tell you later,' he said, staring ahead at the road through the clunking wipers and driving rain.

The rain became heavier and the road steeper.

We were half-way up a slippery incline when we stopped. In the middle of the road was a chunky stone that blocked our way. Since I was sitting in the passenger seat near the front door, it was my task to get out and shift it. So I opened the door, stepped out and walked towards the stone as the pelting rain plucked and teased the surface of every sepia pool. I hefted it end-over-end towards the edge of the road, then, with muddy hands and soaking back, passed through headlight beams that were pierced with glistening little spears of plummeting rain.

I quickly opened the car door and slipped back into my seat. In a few moments we were on our way again.

After another half-hour we passed a little village of oblong stone buildings, some with exterior staircases running up diagonally to their flat roofs. Each dwelling had its own huge conical dunghill neatly stacked and ready for use as winter fuel. Every house was silent and dark.

A little further on, a rough track branched off to our left. Our driver, after some hesitation, decided to take it. It was crossed by deep ruts and in several places was washed out. Our driver slowed down in an effort to ease us through. However, it wasn't long before we bumped down into a deep rut where our back wheels began to spin. We were stuck in the mud. We all climbed out to lighten the load; our driver revved the engine. The wheels spun and went down into the mud like circular saws. It was time for us all to push.

So in the pouring rain, with our hair streaming down over our foreheads and our shirts transparent and clinging to our skin with sharp thin creases, we bounced and pushed the little car out.

It was a procedure that was to be repeated a number of times during the next half hour.

'He's taking us all over these mountains to confuse us,' said Ron.

By the time we'd travelled on for another forty minutes, I was fairly sure that Ron was right.

It was getting on towards 11 o'clock when we came to the crest of a slope. There ahead of us were the distant lights of a large town.

'Bingol?' I asked our driver.

He nodded. I wondered how he planned to release us. If he drove us right into town, he'd be running the risk of being apprehended by the local constabulary or army. Even if he ventured on to the local roads around the town, it would be risky. I wondered whether he might be planning to set us down near some outlying village. Perhaps he might even drop us off a little way along this road, leaving us to make our own way into town.

He came to another small crossroads and, instead of heading down towards the lights of Bingol, veered off again. As we made this detour the lights were obscured and did not reappear until we had covered many more miles. When they did, they were further away than they had been before. We were certainly getting 'the grand tour'.

I decided to sound our driver out on the idea of depositing us at some hotel.

'*Bir otel*—Bingol?' I asked.

'*Bir otel?*' he queried.

'*Evet,*' I replied, pointing to all of us to indicate that we wanted a place to stay.

'*Bu gece,*' added Gary, stressing that we needed the hotel tonight.

Our driver gave us the name of a hotel. Gary and I repeated it, then I asked the driver whether it was a good one.

'*Cok guzel?*' I inquired.

'*Cok cok guzel!*' he responded, with an enthusiastic hand gesture that reinforced his response that it was a very, very good hotel.

Of course, the fellow hadn't said he was taking us to this place in his taxi. All he had done was tell us the name of a place where we could be well accommodated—as any obliging local might do.

Although Gary's and my conversation with him had been shouted, the roar of the engine and the drumming of the rain made it virtually impossible for Ron, Marvin and Richard to hear it from the back seat. So I relayed the information to them in an effort to keep them informed.

At last, we began to come down the mountain towards the lights of the town. It was a tortuous descent that took us around the steep side of a large valley. The engine roared as our driver used his low gears to avoid brake-fade on the steep sections. He had a lot of trouble engaging third gear. When we came down into the foothills, we drove through several more villages. Again, there were no lights in their turf-roofed dwellings and no sign of the people who lived in them. The road was also completely deserted.

The rain eased off as we left the foothills behind and headed towards the outskirts of the town. In a matter of minutes we came to a sealed road. A sign pointed to the right. It said 'Bingol'. Our driver ignored it and drove straight on.

'Bingol?' I asked urgently as I pointed back to the place where he ought to have turned.

Our driver shook his head. He seemed agitated. When Gary asked him why he was not taking us into Bingol, he told him there were too many police on that road.

Unfortunately, none of our back-seat passengers was able to hear this because of the roar of the engine as it was forced to cope with the gap between second and fourth gear. Understandably, they were puzzled and not a little annoyed by the fact that we had not taken the turning to Bingol.

Our driver kept watching out for other vehicles as he glanced in his rear-vision mirror and scanned the side streets.

We approached a T-junction. There was a service-station to our right and in the fork ahead a brightly lit motel. In front of it were several parked cars.

Our driver gave no indication that he was about to stop, and simply began to veer to the left.

'Stop here!' shouted Ron.

The driver did not respond.

'Stop here!' Ron shouted again.

There was still no response as the car sped on into the darkness. Suddenly, Ron lunged forward. Reaching over the driver's shoulders, he wrenched the steering wheel sharply to the left. With a screech of tyres the car swerved across the road, lurched down through a gutter and careered towards a clump of trees.

The driver jerked the wheel back—and the car shot up on to the road again. It was about to tip and roll when the driver twirled the wheel again and somehow managed to keep it upright.

As the vehicle stabilised, he shook his head.

'Tch-tch-tch,' he said with a mixture of anger and frustration.

He was clearly very nervous now but quite determined to drive on. He rammed his gear-lever into second gear then raced the engine in order to jump the gap across into fourth. The motor roared as he rode the clutch.

'Tch-tch-tch...' he lamented, as he shook his head again.

It was now apparent, from his clenched jaw and the veins that stood out on his neck, that the man was almost beside himself with fear.

The PKK had given him the most dangerous job he'd probably ever had—to drive the five of us down from the mountains and deposit us in a town swarming with a record number of Turkish soldiers and police. He was probably aware that at any moment he could be apprehended or even killed. How could he avoid such an encounter? The Turkish authorities could be anywhere—hiding in side streets, behind trees or driving towards him. They could have been parked near the service station or at the motel we'd just passed, in which case they were probably following us right now and using their radio-control to monitor and entrap us.

Our car sped on into the night. No one spoke. The motor roared and the gears grated as our driver made several abortive attempts to change down.

The unspoken question was: Where was he taking us?

It was Gary who verbalised it.

'Nereye gidiyoruz?' he asked.

'Hammamlar' our driver replied, naming some local village.

'Kilometres ne kadar?' Gary queried.

'Alti kilometres,' he answered tensely, without turning his head.

After about five minutes we reached the crest of a hill and we saw the village about a kilometre down the road.

'There it is,' I said to Gary. 'His estimate was about right.'

I turned to our back-seat passengers.

'This looks like the place where he'll drop us off,' I said, pointing ahead to the tiny settlement that nestled down the road in the valley.

Suddenly, the interior of our car was flooded with almost blinding light. It came from the headlights of a truck parked on the side of the road ahead of us. The lights flicked off, then on again. We were being signalled to stop.

Our driver made no response.

The lights flicked off and on again. I was certain it was a police truck.

Our driver evidently thought so too. He accelerated past the truck towards the village.

The place was deserted, but as we drove between the old stone buildings, I noticed some cars parked beside the road on our left. When we drew nearer, our driver scrutinised them carefully; then, after a furtive glance in his rear-vision mirror, sped on through the village.

The fellow was almost beside himself with fear as he headed towards a little bridge at the bottom of the slope.

'He's taking us back along the road to Erzurum!' boomed Ron, 'to the place where we were captured!'

'We're getting out here!' Ron shouted, opening the rear-left door and flinging it wide.

The driver applied his brakes just short of the bridge, but did not stop.

'We're getting out!' shouted Ron again and began to do it.

The car came to a standstill—just beyond the bridge. We all hastily climbed out.

As I slammed the front door, I caught a glimpse of the driver. His eyes were wild with fear as he engaged the gears and revved the motor. In a matter of seconds he was speeding towards the brow of the hill and was soon lost to view behind it. I wondered, as the sound of his engine dwindled to a distant high-pitched hum, whether he'd be able to elude the police or even survive the night.

How quiet it was as Gary and I turned and walked back towards the bridge! Ron, Marvin and Richard had already crossed over it and were heading into the village.

I glanced at my watch. It was almost midnight.

'Hope we can find a phone somewhere,' I said to Gary as I tried to cushion my leg against the hardness of the bitumen with my stick.

'Can't see one,' said Gary. 'And there's no one to ask.'

'They're all in bed,' I added, glancing at the locked doors and windows that communicated nothing and welcomed nobody.

My inane comment was the product of a weary mind that had become accustomed to freewheeling along the hostage highway. For three weeks, I'd been given no opportunity to formulate any plans that might lead to meaningful decisions. Having lived at gun-point for this period, I had learned to stifle the kind of thinking that might prompt me to take the initiative—and I'd become used to it.

I was beginning to understand how difficult it must be for someone who has been imprisoned for a long time and then released, to grasp the fact that he is actually free and then begin to think and behave as though he is.

What would be our next move? We were about to discover that the next move was not ours either.

Ron, Marvin and Richard had been stopped by two men. They were standing next to one of the parked cars we had passed as we drove through the village. Gary and I were about to join them when two men sitting in another vehicle approached us. They were dressed in the green and brown leopard-spot battle-dress worn by the Eastern Turkish police. One of them, a young man of about thirty years of age, carried a two-way radio. We asked him in Turkish whether he would take us to a hotel in Bingol. He did not answer, but laid the little antennaed radio against the side of his head and began to initiate a conversation with someone—presumably at police headquarters—in Turkish.

Within a minute or so, the five of us were on our way to Bingol. Gary and I sat silently in the back seat until we pulled up outside Bingol Police Station.

Although it was well after midnight, the place was alive with activity. We climbed out of the car and walked up the front steps. The glass doors were deferentially opened for us by young policemen who wore mottled army uniforms and tightly-laced gaiters.

They stood back with stiff military formality as we entered the foyer and headed upstairs. On the first floor we were motioned into a large room where the Chief of Police, a balding middle-aged man, was engaged in a telephone conversation behind his desk. Like everyone else, he was dressed in paramilitary attire. As we entered, he pressed the phone to his chest then smiled warmly, leaned across his desk to shake our hands, and asked us to sit down. He continued his phone call as we were served *çay* and Coca Cola. After about ten minutes, the Chief put down his phone, then through an interpreter began to talk with us about the kidnapping.

From that moment, we were swept along on a stream of events that continued to flow until we left Turkey—and which, in fact, continued to flow more than a year later. We were asked to supply as much information as we could to enable the police to locate and apprehend our captors. In addition to being asked numerous questions about the guerrillas, their activities and hiding places, we were invited to examine a large wall-map to identify the mountain route we had followed by foot and then by car prior to our release.

While all this was going on, a local doctor was brought in to examine Richard's hand and my leg. He provided some preliminary treatment in the form of antibiotic cream for Richard and lotion for me.

Then the American and British diplomats arrived and began to speak with the other four men in our group. I was told that Allen Williams, the Australian Consul, would not be here to speak with me. He had gone back to Ankara only the day before we arrived. Apparently, as soon as our capture was made public, the Australian Embassy in Ankara had arranged for Allen and another diplomat to travel to Bingol, where they had stayed for almost the entire period until now. I was assured that these two men had been wonderfully supportive and helpful throughout the entire period that we were missing.

Next, we were permitted to make brief international phone calls to our families.

When I phoned Margaret, she recognised my voice, but at first found it difficult to grasp the fact that the husband whom she had accepted might possibly be dead was now speaking to her.

'Is that you, Allen?' she asked in tremulous disbelief.

The sound of her voice somehow convinced me that at last I was free.

'Yes, it is,' I replied. 'We're at Bingol Police Station and we're all OK.'

'How is your ankle?' she asked.

'It's pretty swollen,' I answered. 'A bit of phlebitis caused by our heavy mountain trekking. But it's OK. We're all fine.'

I told her that this had to be a brief call and that I would phone again later. I added that I was thankful to God for our

release, and that we were grateful for the many people who had prayed for us. I asked how she and the family were and assured them of my love. I finished by telling her I would be returning to Australia as soon as possible.

Meanwhile, late as it was, a number of local reporters and photographers began to arrive to cover our release. It was not until 3.30 am that we were taken to the Chief of Police's house, where arrangements had been made for us to spend the rest of the night.

I will never forget the moment in his bathroom when I was about to wash myself, and suddenly became aware of the terrible stench of my body. Nor will I forget the repugnance with which I stuffed all my clothing into a large plastic laundry bag, then lathered and scrubbed my entire body with almost pathological persistence for the next ten minutes.

After barely three hours' restless sleep—during which time I failed miserably to make the adjustment from hard ground to soft mattress—I was up and on my way again, with the others, to Police Headquarters.

By eight o'clock, breakfast was under way, and with it, another host of questions. The questions continued through most of the morning. We were asked to make not only spoken responses but also written ones, in questionnaires and signed statements. All of this was legally necessary, we were told, to enable further action to be taken by the authorities on our behalf. Although the procedure was lengthy and wearying, it soon became apparent that this was much more than some bureaucratic formality. Nor was it a perfunctory political gesture to placate our governments. Those in charge were obviously concerned about what had happened to us. While I was dictating my personal statement, the young man typing it told me that a number of his friends in the army and the police force had been recently killed by the PKK.

As the morning programme continued, I began to understand a little better the position of those charged with maintaining the rule of law in Eastern Turkey. Most of them had in some way experienced the suffering or death brought by terrorism. Consequently, they quickly identified with people like us who had also known something of these things. It had become personal for them, and for each one of the thousands of men involved in searching for us who had put their lives on the line to rescue us.

The morning programme was interspersed with other activities. A panel of doctors from Bingol Hospital examined me but failed to diagnose what was later ascertained by ultrasound at Westmead Hospital in Australia; that I did have a venous thrombosis, a clot in my leg.

A full press conference was held. As a result, news of our release—and, of course, our Nuh'un Gemisi project—were rapidly spread world-wide.

About noon, we were told that a helicopter would be arriving shortly to take us on a journey to Incirlik, a Turkish/United States military base, for a short period of rest and recuperation. We had seen many helicopters during the past three weeks, but this one was different. As it hovered overhead, we were sure its pilot knew exactly where we were and was indeed coming down to get us.

We thanked the Chief of Police and others who had taken such good care of us since our release, and checked our baggage before it was loaded. My belongings consisted of just one tightly sealed bag of soiled clothing. Everything I was wearing had been kindly lent me by Marvin, except for a new pair of shoes which Ron, with typical generosity, had bought for me from a Bingol shoe-salesman by special arrangement with the Chief of Police.

In a few minutes more the five of us, together with our British and American diplomats, were snugly seated in the passenger cabin. With an engine roar that made our intestines vibrate, we lifted off. A dust-whirling blast of air fluttered the hair and clothes of those who stood below. Their bodies foreshortened and diminished as we lifted, then tilted and slipped away—from them, the police station and Bingol town.

Within a minute, we were flying over the mountains where we had been held as prisoners. We saw the dark massive bulk of the huge wave-like mountain that had so menaced me on our first night in Black Hell Valley. The emotions I had experienced that night began to flood back as I surveyed those precipitous slopes and that awesome gorge. Black Hell Valley disappeared slowly beneath us. The mountains beyond stretched to the horizon, their bald brown undulations blotched with the blue-black shadows of clouds. I looked down at the thin patches of oak scrub scattered here and there.

'They're down there somewhere...' I said to myself as I gazed down between the trees. 'Ibrahim, Dilah and the rest of them. Some will be sleeping. Others will be performing their daily camp routines.' I wondered whether Kocak and his group were with them. The young students who had been doing their PKK 'national service' would be down there somewhere too, heading towards their homes and the next term of school or university.

As I watched ridge after ridge pass below me, I realised what a hopeless task it must have seemed to those who had been searching for us over these past three weeks...

'Strewth, mate, you had us all worried there for a bit,' said Allen Williams, the Australian Consul, as he shook my hand in Ankara.

After our three days in Incirlik I had come to Ankara to meet Allen and the Ambassador, to pick up my luggage and—perhaps most important of all—to discuss with Turkish Government officials the matter of our dig permit for next year.

On the evening of Tuesday 24 September, having completed a number of television, radio and press interviews, I was relaxing with Allen in his Embassy apartment. We had just enjoyed a wonderful Thai meal cooked by his wife.

Allen leaned forward and tapped the long cylindrical ash from his cigarette.

'I've got some good news and some bad news for you, Al,' he said. 'I thought it would be better to wait until you'd finished your meal before I told you.'

'What is it?' I asked.

He leaned back and drew on his cigarette.

'The good news is that a number of the terrorists who took you hostage have been caught and shot. The bad news is that the newspaper that reported it says it was the information given by you guys that enabled the police to track 'em down and shoot 'em.

'As you can see,' he said stubbing his cigarette then handing me the newspaper, 'they printed all your names too—which makes you a sitting duck for terrorists. We've been instructed by Canberra to get you out of the country before somebody takes a pot-shot at you. Now you've been on national and international television, you'll be easily recognised. So just to be on the safe side, we'll cancel your return flight to London and put you on another airline tomorrow...'

As I listened to Allen explaining these plans to get me out of Turkey, my thoughts refused to stay on track. Allen's voice began to recede; it had that strange far-away shallowness that voices have when the listener is very tired and fighting to stay awake and concentrate.

Only key phrases registered. 'Arrange for you to re-route through Frankfurt'...'afternoon flight'...'under no circumstances leave the Embassy...'

I was back in the mountains now, my mind dominated by one insistent question: 'Who has been killed?'

The question kept breaking on the beach of my mind—waves from a strange dark sea of sadness.

Had any of those tragically misguided youngsters been killed?

Perhaps the little thirteen-year-old girl?

Perhaps her friend Silan—poor Silan, vulnerable and sexually abused, her way to real love barred now and for ever by death.

Maybe Çia was dead? Çia, the Marxist university student. Of course it was different for Çia. Like most of the others, he was older and knew what he was doing. Furthermore, Çia was an intellectual who had chosen terrorism, knowing full well what dreadful things it would involve for him and those he helped recruit.

In my mind I saw the gloomy interior of a makeshift mortuary. In it lay the bodies of Kocak, the bushy-bearded fire-worshipper; Dilah, the ideologue, her khaki uniform no longer immaculate, but stained red-brown with blood. And Ibrahim, once the general, but now just another face to weep over in someone else's PKK album of dead would-be Kurdish heroes.

Good news?

Terrorism is wrong whatever its motives, whatever its guise. It has its fearful price and that price had been paid. Law and order had been upheld—at terrible cost. Many Turkish soldiers had been shot by the PKK too. The fact that I had not known *them* personally did not make their deaths any the less tragic. Every one of them was someone's brother, son, husband...

My eyes grew hot with tears—tears that blurred the distinction between guerrilla and soldier, between Kurd and non-Kurd.

Inwardly I wept for the people of a land I had come to love.

CHAPTER

11

Tumult and Shouting

Wednesday afternoon, 25 September: I was on a Lufthansa jet, *en route* to London via Frankfurt.

Gary was at some undisclosed destination, at last enjoying the holiday which had been so annoyingly interrupted several weeks ago. Ron, Richard and Marvin had doubtless been reunited with their families for some days.

Our little team had been well and truly broken up. Of course I had little doubt that I would be in continuing contact with Ron and the others, especially since my recent discussions with Turkish Ministry officials about our 1992 dig permit had been so encouraging. I was sure we'd be back together again within a year or so.

Ongoing contact with Gary seemed less likely, I thought, even though he had invited us to share a special Turkish reunion meal with him some time in London. I had told him that if this nostalgic meal were to be an authentic culinary re-creation complete with goat's liver, then regardless of how attractive it might be to Marvin, I'd be giving it a miss.

As we gained altitude, I leaned back and began to relax.

I remembered Gary on that first night. 'Poor old Gary,' I thought. 'What a shock to his system it must have been, having just emerged from a nervous breakdown! As though being whisked away by Kurdish guerrillas were not enough; but then to discover that his only English-speaking companions were four fellows who thought that Noah's ark might still exist and were actually out looking for it. Surely that must have been the ultimate test of any man's sanity!' Yet Gary had passed this and every other test with flying colours. Up to this point, we all had done so, it seemed, though only time would tell.

The doctors and psychiatrists who had checked us out at Incirlik certainly thought so. The hospital chaplain had told us that in the staff's opinion, the five of us were in remarkably good shape, considering what had happened to us. Even the briefest of skirmishes with life-threatening danger can do long-term damage to the personality. The bank teller or the storekeeper who is suddenly faced by an armed robber, even for a few seconds, can sometimes be so traumatised that years of counselling are needed to restore his shattered behaviour patterns.

Somehow, we had escaped all that. And I couldn't help feeling as I sat there in the plane that was flying me home that we had all been preserved, not only physically, but psychologically, in a special if not supernatural way. My mind leapt back to a discussion we'd had with a young sandy-haired chaplain, whilst we lounged about on our hospital beds one afternoon. As we had chatted together, a number of us had told him that in our opinion the reason we'd come through the experience so well was that many people had continuously prayed for us. I had added that I had personally sensed this and had in fact discussed it with the other men at the time. The chaplain had noticed that Gary, who was lying on his bed, was not contributing to the conversation.

'Hey, Gary,' he'd asked, 'how did you get on with these four guys when they talked about spiritual things?'

'I just switched off,' Gary had replied, with an impish grin.

I remembered how we'd all laughed at his remark. Yet beneath the joviality that comes so easily when men have been through a lot together, there was an unspoken awareness that a spiritual dynamic had been operating throughout the entire situation. I sensed then that we really had survived the ordeal, and that we would in fact all be stronger because of it.

I reclined my seat, closed my eyes and quietly thanked God for preserving us and asked that he would indeed strengthen us and use all that had happened for his own purposes.

After a short stay in London I returned to Australia. My reunion with Margaret and my family at Sydney airport was no private matter. The image of a smiling lady being hugged by a

Mirror

WIN A
SPRING
CLEAN
Page 8

'... the moon'

Ark man savors freedom

● Home at last .... Dr Roberts reunited with his wife, Margaret.

AUSTRALIAN archeologist Dr Allen Roberts, taken hostage by Kurdish rebels in Turkey last month, was reunited with his family in Sydney yesterday.

Dr Roberts, 59, had spent three weeks camping in freezing conditions with his kidnappers.

"I am delighted to finally be home. I feel absolutely marvellous," he said.

"I am looking forward to trimming my beard and sleeping in a bed."

Dr Roberts also gave details about his expedition to find Noah's Ark.

He, his three fellow explorers and a tourist were

abducted on August 30 and taken into mountains near Ararat — the site of their archeological dig — by the rebels.

"At first we didn't know if we were going to be shot because there was a lot of gun waving and shouting going on," Dr Roberts said.

"But after a couple of minutes they started handing out clothing and we knew we would be all right."

Dr Roberts developed frostbite in several toes and it was this which led to the group's release on September 21.

The Kurds free group after consider Roberts' condition

Dr Roberts was day excited about t honorary work.

"We have a boat ... which is the same as Noah's Ark is in the right pl..

"All indications h Turkish Govern show they wou pleased to have us next year."

Measurements of t Ark given in the matched those o fossilised structur... said.

● Margaret and daughter Anne celebrate his ...ctor's grandchildren Neil, Erin and Linden

Thank God I'm free, says doctor

SYDNEY DOCTOR KIDNAP

...walked the remaining few kilometres to the tiny village of Bingol, ...kilom from Anasrk where he used a pay phone to call his wife in Sydney.

"I'm okay. I've got a badly swollen ankle from walking around the mountains for three weeks, but I'm okay," Dr Roberts assured his wife Margaret during a brief telephone conversation.

"We are all well, we have been fed well and treated respectfully. The only problem is my ankle will need treatment, but

thank God I'm free," he said.

A Turkish army spokesman in Bingol told the Sunday Telegraph that the rebels had kidnapped Dr Roberts by mistake, believing he was an American.

The spokesman said Dr Roberts was unhurt and would be returning to Australia as soon as possible.

His relieved wife told the Sunday Telegraph she was apparently unaware of the attention his captivity had received around the world.

The Roberts family and the Australian Gov...

...EED ARK MA... ...EN TO RETUR...

HUNT FO...

NOAH'S A...

HOSTAG...

...CURRIE ...ALIAN ...gist Dr ...ts is keen ...his search ...rk despite ...n held by ...kidnappers ...weeks.

● Dr Roberts ...

● Mrs Roberts ... supports new search.

...f wife. Mar... ...yesterday ev...

...pected her hust ...torn to Austr... week.

She said the o... other freed arc... Mrs Mary Nell W... learnt the group r... made to walk to camps each night.

"They were in caves and under ... Mrs Roberts said.

"They had been ... and the water did b... aggr... with them.

bushy-bearded man wearing a leather jacket and broad-brimmed hat was captured in a blaze of flashlights by the Australian media. To a round of loud applause, I gave Margaret a box of orchids I had bought in Singapore. Then to my surprise it was my turn to receive some flowers. They came in the form of a goodwill 'welcome home' gesture from two young girls dressed in national Kurdish costume.

After a brief reunion with my children, my grandchildren and many friends, I went with Margaret into the airport Press Conference room. I began by expressing my thanks to those who had been so concerned for me during the time I had been a hostage. I thanked the media in particular for its contribution, which I had learned was far more than simply reporting news as it came to hand but included keeping my wife and family informed and on occasions actually encouraging them when things looked bad. This, I said, was the Australian media at its best. Then came the questions.

Although this was my first media interview on Australian soil, it was not radically different from interviews I had given from overseas by telephone and television satellite. The pattern of questions was essentially the same. It usually began with a round of queries about the kidnapping, the first ones focusing upon how it happened and what I thought and felt about it all. There were generally questions too about the danger aspect: 'Did you ever think you might lose your life?' 'What were your thoughts and feelings at such times?' The question of why we were taken hostage was also part of this segment of questions.

Once the hostage questions were over, the Noah's ark questions would begin. Among the first of these would usually be something like:

'Dr Roberts, I understand you were in Turkey examining a large boat-shaped object that could be Noah's ark. Do you believe it is Noah's ark?'

I was aware even before our release that such a question would be asked. And I also knew that as an historian whose primary aim was to gather, assess and present evidence, I had to be very careful about how such a question was answered. So to the question 'Do you believe it is Noah's ark?' I would often respond by saying, 'The question is not really a matter of belief, but of evidence. What I believe, or what you believe, is not really the issue. What is actually under that mud is the issue.'

It was not an attempt to be deceptive or avoid the real issue but to confront it. Usually this response moved the interview away from the subjective area of what Roberts personally believed into the much more profitable area of verifiable evidence. As a result, the interviewer would then ask a question about evidence, which I would try to answer with the data which suggested that under this mud, at an altitude of some 6,300 feet, were some of the structures one might expect to find in a gigantic ancient boat. In the course of further questioning I tried, whenever I could, to point out that a good deal of evidence had been found as a result of high-tech subsurface investigations carried out by very competent researchers — several of them university scientists whose work had been sponsored under Turkish Government authority.

Most of my interviewers knew that I was hoping to return to Turkey. I was usually asked whether I was afraid that if I did go back, I might be in danger again. My answer to that question was that the data amassed so far raised questions which could be fully answered only by an excavation, and that those of us who wanted to see the job done would have to go back regardless of the difficulties or dangers. I usually stressed that I was not the discoverer of the formation and also that I was only one member of a team co-operating with the Turkish authorities to ensure the excavation, protection and development of the site.

Media interest ran high for months following my return. Friends of mine who were journalists said that this was not surprising, for the story had all the right ingredients: the hostages whose families did not know for weeks whether their loved ones were alive or dead; the trauma of it all, followed by the emotional re-unions after their loved ones' release; and of course the quest to investigate an archaeological site that many believed might possibly be Noah's ark.

Media coverage was so wide that people would approach Margaret and myself when we went into shopping centres and restaurants. They were invariably friendly and keen to know whether I would be going back to dig the site. I recall that one day I was a passenger in a taxi. When we stopped at some traffic-lights a car pulled up in the lane next to us. The driver wound down his window and made signs for me to do the same. I thought that perhaps he had noticed something wrong with our vehicle and was doing the neighbourly thing of telling us. I wound my window down, whereupon he gave me the Aussie thumbs up 'She'll be right' sign and shouted 'Good on yer, mate! Hope yer can get back to Turkey and prove it!'

These expressions of genuine interest, together with an inundation of phone calls and letters, were indications that the subject had evoked in the ordinary Australian an interest that I had not anticipated.

I have often wondered what it was that prompted and still prompts such widespread interest in the subject of Noah's ark. Quite apart from the fact that the account of the flood and the ark is universally known, I wondered whether there might be another reason—something rather more subtle. The ark is a symbol of survival and safety in a world which many fear is destined for disaster. Perhaps for those who see in today's world the apocalyptic signs of impending global destruction, oxygen and water depletion, pollution and ozone layer problems, there has to be an

Victorian newspaper cartoon following 40 days of continuous rain (*Reproduced by permission of the* Herald-Sun, *Melbourne*)

ark—some means of preserving life on this planet, some means of survival and safety.

Over the next few months, Ron and I in our respective countries began to initiate plans through the appropriate authorities to see the project continued in the following summer. The Turkish Embassies were, as usual, most helpful. However, the process was slowed down in Turkey itself as result of ministerial changes following an election there. Added to this was the uncertainty of the political situation around Turkey's eastern borders. Nevertheless the necessary plans and applications were made to enable us to move towards a preliminary dig in the summer of 1992.[1]

Early in that year it was decided that an Australia-wide tour should be organised. To this end I prepared a lecture illustrated with colour transparencies. My aim was to present a range of visual and other evidence from the Akyayla site with a summary of its history and development to date. I had been encouraged by the intelligent interest the subject had aroused all over the country and even overseas. This had been clearly evidenced by the letters and phone-calls which had been pouring in for months. Many people had made arrangements to come to my home to discuss ideas and information related to the project.

Those who contacted me represented a most interesting cross-section: academic and non-academic, religious and non-religious. We were impressed not only by the wide interest the subject seemed to have evoked, but by the thoughtfulness of so many of the responses, some of which confronted us with issues and new lines of thinking we had never previously considered. I was encouraged by the possibility that a national tour might stimulate further information and ideas.

The question, for example, of what is 'gopher' wood had prompted some very stimulating responses. The term had puzzled many for a long time. The more generally accepted notion was probably that it was a species of wood such as cyprus.[2] However, recent research into the matter had produced a number of very interesting ideas, one of which was that gopher might not be a kind or species of wood at all, but might be a *process*— lamination. Ron had already suggested that layers on the 'deck-timber' sample he was permitted to retrieve from the site were laminations. Then in mid-1991 a friend of mine, Dr Ronald Charles, supplied me with a very interesting piece of information on the subject. Dr Charles, a scientist who had been engaged in archaeological research for several years, told me that when he had been in Saudi Arabia he was talking with an Arab who used a word that sounded like 'gopher'. Dr Charles, who was not fluent in the language, tried to find out what the word meant. After a frustrating time of reciprocal miming followed by much shaking and nodding of heads, it became clear that the word did indeed refer to wood—but not a particular sort of wood. It was a process, a fact that finally became clear when the Arab laid the palm of one down-turned hand upon the top of his other hand and repeated the word 'gophering'.

Had this word, and the process it appeared to represent, survived down through the millennia to surface in this recognisable form now, in the twentieth century?[3]

Having shared this incident in the course of a lecture I gave in Great Britain, a lady who had been teaching dressmaking in a technical college came up to me and asked, 'Do you know what a "goffering" machine is?' I told her I hadn't the faintest idea, so she went on to explain that it was a machine which had been used for centuries to layer or pleat materials—skirts, kilts and Elizabethan ruffles.

Those of us who are academics need to be reminded from time to time that we can all too easily become victims of our own specialisation. Sometimes, the most useful leads in research are opened up by people who make no claims to expertise in the particular field in which the academic specialist is working. In research, one needs balance—breadth as well as depth.

Perhaps there is some truth in the jibe that specialists can be in danger of learning more and more about less and less, until they know everything about nothing. As I prepared my lecture for the tour, I looked forward to having a wide range of people appraise the evidence, then intelligently respond to it.

Through a series of state co-ordinators, preparations were made to organise a public lecture itinerary that would take me to all Australian capital cities. The first of these lecture meetings was held in Adelaide, South Australia, on 1 April 1992. It was attended by almost 1,000 people. Our next meeting the following night was attended by about 800.

Because we wanted to make the lecture available to as many people as possible, our entry fee was very small, almost nominal—

four Australian dollars per person, with a special reduction for families and students. It was hoped that further interest would be encouraged through video and audio tapes of the lecture as well as a small booklet, all of which were to be available for sale following each meeting. It was our publicly stated intention that any monies raised from the sale of these items, from donations and from entrance fees, would be used to assist in financing the work necessary to investigate and develop the site.

Both media and public response were very positive as we left Adelaide and headed for Melbourne, Victoria.

Little did any of us realise what was being planned for our major lecture in that city and for other meetings to follow.

The guerrilla operation that made me a hostage for three hazardous weeks in Turkey was in some respects mild compared with the campaign that was about to be launched that night in Australia. Over the next several months, our major meetings were disrupted by individuals and groups of academics. These incidents were then taken up in the Press and the media Australia-wide. In the process I came under heavy personal attack.

For example, attempts were made to discredit me by calling me 'a self-proclaimed archaeologist', when I had gone to considerable lengths to explain that my university training was not in archaeology but history. It is perfectly normal, of course, for historians to be involved in archaeological research. Archaeology today is multi-faceted and specialised, requiring research in many disciplines. Hence those involved in a project might be scientists of various kinds, anthropologists, geographers and historians. And depending on the nature of the project, many, even most of them, often possess no formal archaeological training. The joint research project conducted on the Akyayla site in July 1987, involving Ataturk University and Los Alamos National Laboratory of the University of California under the authority of the Turkish Prime Minister, provides an excellent example of this. The two leaders were both scientists, not archaeologists. The majority of the team were not archaeologists either.[4]

The history of archaeology furnishes many similar examples and in fact reveals that some of the most important discoveries have been made by people who had no academic qualifications at all: a goatherd discovered the Dead Sea Scrolls.

Doubts were also raised about the legitimacy of the academic qualifications I do hold,[5] and further doubts were raised about the authenticity of the evidence I had presented, including my photographs.[6] Finally, although our kidnapping had been one of the most widely reported incidents of that kind for many years, doubt was cast upon that too.[7]

Our honeymoon with the Press and media appeared to be over.

Disappointing as it was to find such irresponsibility in sections of our Australian Press, the most worrying aspect of it all for those of us involved was that the focus of public attention was being shifted away from the evidence we were presenting. The real issue of whether there were sufficient indications that the formation should be excavated was almost lost in a welter of assaults on my personal credibility.

It soon became apparent that certain members of the opposing scientific establishment were making the rounds of radio stations and newspapers where I had been interviewed. Whilst I had no objection to their voicing their opposition in this manner, I found the quality of their responses very disappointing. They rarely, if ever, addressed the scientific evidence I had cited.

It was hard to believe that our public presentation, after only a few months, had aroused such extraordinary antagonism. We had seen our evidence sneered at or dismissed without examination by a range of academics. A widespread media campaign had been organised to oppose us. Our public meetings had been disrupted mainly by academics, some of whom had to be removed by the police for disturbing the peace. Then, flying a 'freedom of speech' flag, sections of the Press had complained that we were the aggressors. Throughout the entire period, my wife and I had been receiving abusive mail.

In spite of all this opposition, those of us involved in the work resolved to continue with our tour, our research programme and our arrangements to ensure that the site be excavated at the earliest opportunity. We continued to be convinced that a properly organised preliminary dig would provide the archaeological confirmation needed to settle the question of whether the formation was a boat or not. We also held firmly to the opinion that if a positive identification of the formation as a boat were established, then subsequent more extensive excavation should establish and confirm *which* boat or *whose* boat it was.

Since its inception, we had steadfastly maintained that there was enough evidence of anomalous features on the site to suggest that the formation was not a natural one and warranted excavation. Should the formation turn out to be a natural one after all, both I and those involved in the project would be quick to say so and would say it publicly. Successful research is not simply a matter of looking for evidence to prop up some preconceived assumption. It involves finding out what is there and then seeking honestly to interpret it, in the hope of determining its significance.

Those of us in Australia and overseas who are committed to seeing the site properly excavated, protected and appropriately developed have firmly resolved not to be put off by those who oppose us. The shouting of academics and others, who have made up their minds without having been to the site or having even examined the evidence, will not change the fact that there is a gigantic boat-shaped formation in the mountains of Eastern Turkey that needs to be excavated. The evidence concerning what it is does not lie within men's opinions. It lies within the formation itself, under the mud that covers it there on that Turkish mountain range.

People all over Australia know this. The Australian is neither naive nor gullible. He has developed over a couple of centuries of pioneering his country a healthy disrespect for those who are all theory and no practice. He is refreshingly pragmatic and marvellous at solving problems in the most practical and direct way. If you have a problem and want it fixed, an Aussie may well do it for you with a bit of fencing wire. The theoretical pontifications of self-styled experts do not greatly impress him—especially if he suspects they have some hidden agenda. It did not take long for those Australians who attended my lectures to size up the people who set out to disrupt them. At our Sydney meeting one of the disrupters shouted out, 'Listen to us—we're the academics!' to which one of the audience replied, 'Then why don't you act like them?'—a rejoinder that brought forth a burst of rollicking laughter across the auditorium from the majority of the audience.

Many of those who witnessed this disruptive element in action wrote letters to the Press. Several asked why a lecture of this kind should provoke such violent reaction. One such letter, published in *The Australian* of 25 May 1992 stated:

I had previously no contact with Dr Roberts or the organisation supporting him, but went along out of interest to hear what he had to say. He was very balanced and cautious in some of the conclusions that could be gained from research thus far.

However we were very upset towards the end of the meeting when a group of 20 or so people came in and sat down and started to heckle him and would not stop even though it was obvious from the many hundreds in the auditorium they were not welcome and were asked to stop. Of the small group, some claimed to be intellectuals, experts and academics—I don't know who they were. The fact that they would not let Dr Roberts finish his evening uninterrupted upset me and many others very much.

All I can surmise is that Dr Roberts must be on to something very important...

If these interjectors are teachers at our universities then no wonder the standard of graduates in some faculties leaves much to be desired. Whatever happened to freedom of speech, or agreeing to disagree? (Cliff Hollings, Miranda)

Around the same time, a press release made available to the Australian media following one of my disrupted lectures stated, 'Australian historian Dr Allen Roberts, who was captured by Kurdish rebels last year, presented in his Australia-wide tour a wide range of scientific evidence documenting the Turkish Government's claim that there is a large boat-shaped formation which is the length of Noah's ark in the Mountains of Ararat.'[8]

The release went on to say that thousands of people had accepted Dr Roberts's invitation to peruse this evidence, but that 'a small group of people claiming to be scientists [had] repeatedly disregarded the evidence and disrupted [these meetings] shouting Dr Roberts down during question time.'

'A spokesman for the Sydney organisers who made this press release available said, "The behaviour of these academics was childish and angered the vast majority of the audience who gave Dr Roberts a standing ovation when the meeting had to be prematurely closed." '

The press release struck a humorous note when it told how this same spokesman had asked one of the scientists who attended the lecture what he thought Dr Roberts and the archaeological team involved in the forthcoming dig would find there. The answer was, 'A pile of rocks.' The spokesman's shrewd rejoinder was, 'Then why such opposition if that's all he's going to find?'

In 1992, due to further serious political problems in Eastern Turkey and around its borders, it was not possible to carry out the preliminary dig as planned. So we found it necessary to defer it until the summer of 1993. Unfortunately, the same situation continued on into 1993. Killings and kidnappings continued to occur during that year, numbers of them in the region where the formation rests. Any serious attempt to undertake a thorough programme to protect, excavate and develop the site is out of the question until the area is safe again.

Will an excavation of the Akyayla site confirm beyond all doubt that this is the ark of Noah?

Only the excavation itself will bring a conclusive answer to that question.

In the meantime, however, we know that there is enough well-attested evidence to warrant such a dig. Were a positive identification to come forth from it, there is no doubt that the implications would be vast—not only for religion but also for history, science and a range of other disciplines as well. Confirmation that the huge boat-shaped formation is indeed the ark would bring with it several other ramifications—not just about the ark itself, but about the event it was built to withstand: the flood. The same Genesis account that provides us with most of the 'what' and 'where' information we have used to identify the ark, also provides us with important 'what' and 'where' information about the flood.

What it tells us is that the flood was a cataclysm so great that it destroyed all life on the earth, with the exception of those creatures in the ark.

> And all flesh died that moved upon the earth, both of fowl
> and of cattle, and of beast, and of every creeping thing that
> creepeth upon the earth and every man (Gen 7:21).[9]

Where the flood occurred is also set down with the utmost clarity. It is said to have covered the entire planet.

> And the waters prevailed exceedingly upon the earth; and
> all the high hills that were under the whole heaven were
> covered. Fifteen cubits upward did the waters prevail and
> the mountains were covered (Gen 7:19-20).

From a historical perspective, references like these cannot be
ignored, whatever one's opinion of their veracity. They are not
only clear, but central to the whole account that contains them.

The riddle of how a formation that might well be a huge boat
came to be sitting on a mountainside over a mile above sea level is
one that demands a rational answer. If the formation is eventually shown to be the ark of Noah, then the whole question of
how it got there, including the possibility of a flood like the one
described in Genesis, would call for the most serious scientific
and historical consideration.

There would seem to be far more resting on the mountains of
Ararat than a boat-shaped object that could be Noah's ark. In the
realm of religion, that is most certainly the case. The existence of
Noah, the ark and a flood raises questions of fundamental importance concerning God, man and their relationship.

The Genesis account tells us that the flood occurred as a result
of divine judgment on mankind for his wickedness:

> And God saw that the wickedness of man was great in the
> earth, and that every imagination of the thoughts of his
> heart was only evil continually.
> And it repented the Lord that he had made man on the
> earth, and it grieved him at his heart.
> And the Lord said, I will destroy man whom I have created
> from the face of the earth; both man, and beast, and the
> creeping thing, and the fowls of the air; for it repenteth me
> that I have made them (Gen 6:5-7).

Archaeological confirmation of the ark—and, by implication,
the flood—would have a significant influence upon three of the
world's major religions. The account of Noah, the ark and the
flood is common to the teachings of Christianity, Judaism and
Islam. Such information would tend of course to encourage belief
in these things as factual truth. It would almost certainly also
have the effect of causing those who read the ancient writings in

which these things are described to reconsider the question of their historicity. In particular, those who might earlier have relegated Noah, the ark and the flood to the status of myth, legend or religious allegory would need to reappraise their position.

The notion of a pre-flood world that was destroyed by a holy God has been a difficult one for many to accept, as has been the concept of the same God preserving, by means of the ark, a remnant of living things to repopulate the post-flood world. Difficult as all this Old Testament information might be to grasp, its historicity is nevertheless confirmed in the New Testament by Jesus Christ himself. He compares the world-shattering events of Noah, the ark and the flood with another event of world-wide import—his own future return to this earth.

> But as the days of Noah were, so shall also the coming of the Son of Man be.
> For as in the days that were before the flood they were eating and drinking, marrying and giving in marriage, until the day that Noah entered into the ark,
> And knew not until the flood came, and took them all away; so shall also the coming of the Son of Man be (Mt 24:37-39).

It is also interesting to note that the Old Testament teaching about a flood that disrupted the whole of creation is capable of arousing not only unbelief but ignorant antagonism and scoffing—especially when that teaching is related to Christ's second coming. Again in the New Testament, the apostle Peter writes:

> Knowing this first, that there shall come in the last days scoffers, walking after their own lusts, And saying, Where is the promise of his coming? for since the fathers fell asleep, all things continue as they were from the beginning of creation.
> For this they willingly are ignorant of, that by the word of God the heavens were of old, and the earth standing out of the water and in the water:
> Whereby the world that then was, being overflowed with water, perished (2 Pet 3:3-6).

Whatever one thinks of it, the Genesis flood account is a haunting reminder to men and women everywhere that they are accountable to the righteous God who created them.

The Old Testament flood account certainly appears to teach that universal rebellion brings universal judgment and in this sense also teaches the New Testament message that 'the wages of sin is death' (Rom 6:23).

Is it also possible that God's provision of the ark shows that he is willing and able to save man from sin and judgment, and that those who will take him at his word may enter the ark of his salvation?

In this sense, the ark could be seen perhaps as an Old Testament picture of a New Testament reality—Christ, and the salvation he brought when he was crucified, dead, buried and raised again.

> For God so loved the world, that he gave his only begotten Son, that whosoever believeth on him should not perish, but have everlasting life (Jn 3:16).

Perhaps it is also possible that the post-flood world represents the new beginning, the new life that God is able to provide, and according to the Christian faith, has in fact provided in Christ his Son.

> He that believeth on the Son hath everlasting life: and he that believeth not the Son shall not see life; and the wrath of God abideth on him (Jn 3:36).

The quest for Noah's ark brings two challenging questions. The first is archaeological. Could it possibly be that beneath the mud of this huge boat-shaped formation on the mountains of Ararat are the remains of the Noah's ark of Scripture?

Only time will tell.

The second is spiritual and personal. Could it possibly be that regardless of what is under the mud on that mountainside, the message of Noah's ark will cause many of this generation, perhaps even the reader of this book, to trust in a holy God who saves?

Only eternity will tell.

NOTES

1. Necessary discussions and applications were well under way by the beginning of 1992.

2. 'Hebrew and Chaldee Dictionary' in: *Strong's Exhaustive Concordance of the Bible* (nd). Entry 1613: 'gôpher' from an unused root prob. meaning *to house in*; a kind of tree or wood (as used for building) appar. the cypress.

3. That gopher might be plywood is an attractive possibility in that boats have for many centuries utilised plywood. David Fasold however (see *The Ark of Noah*, Wynwood Press: New York NY, 1988, pp 261-273) argues the case for gopher's being KPR—a bituminous mixture of cement which covered a solid reed raft.

4. JULY 1987 GEOPHYSICAL INVESTIGATION OF NOAH'S ARK (DURUPINAR SITE) MAHSER VILLAGE, DOGUBAYAZIT, AGRI. John R. Baumgardner, University of California, Los Alamos National Laboratory. M. Salih Bayraktutan, Ataturk University, Faculty of Engineering, November 1987: Erzurum, Turkey, p 2.

5. The author holds four university degrees; a bachelor's degree from The University of New England, Armidale, NSW (which qualifies him as an historian), two masters degrees, one from Armidale and the other from Sydney University, NSW, and a doctorate from Freedom University in Orlando, Florida, USA. All of these degrees had a significant historical component. All the institutions where these awards were earned are bona fide institutions recognised as such by the states in which they operate. Freedom University is also a seminary which, along with some ninety other non-government institutions in Florida, operates officially and grants legitimate degrees under the appropriate statute. (See letter to Dr A.S. Roberts from The Department of Education, Tallahassee, Florida 32399, dated June 23, 1992 and signed by Charles Davis, Program Specialist of the State Board of Independent Colleges and Universities. This personal letter to the author [under the Great Seal of the State of Florida] states: 'Freedom Seminary [formerly Freedom University] was at the time you attended and is now, along with other religious schools in Florida, legally allowed to operate.' It adds, 'These schools are allowed to offer degrees and graduates are allowed to [legally] use the titles as long as they are in compliance with 817.567 Florida law.') The author holds on file copies of these statutes along with penalties imposed on institutions which, having failed to meet the law, continue to operate and grant degrees and on persons who use the titles (eg. of Dr before their names) illegally.

6. Nearly all of the photographs the author had shown in his lectures had been taken by either Ron Wyatt, his wife or this author. The vast majority the author had taken with his own cameras in triplicate, one complete set with an electronic dating device. These films had been processed and

developed by three reputable Sydney laboratories who signed for them and vouched in writing that they were genuine and had not been tampered with by anyone before or during processing or printing. These laboratories were: Nulab Australia, Castle Hill NSW, Manager P. Briton (colour prints); Vision Graphics, Redfern, NSW, Manager R. Pitman (colour slides), and Steads, Redfern, NSW, Manager E. Stead (black and white).

7. In addition to a vast number of press reports published in Australian and overseas newspapers, the author holds in a 200 page official ɡ ɔvernment file more than 100 documents about the kidnapping. These documents were made available to him through the Freedom of Information Act by courtesy of the Department of Foreign Affairs and Trade in Canberra (Correspondence and annexures 1, 2 and 3 from D.C. Rutter to Roberts, 12 and 17 March 1992). This documentation, along with a range of other evidence, including numerous eye-witness testimonies, clearly establish the hostage-taking as genuine.

8. Press release, May 1992.

9. See also the following two verses: Gen 7:22 and 23.